To our Families

LHASA
TIBET'S FORBIDDEN CITY

by
Frank J. Brignoli
Christine Johnston Brignoli

Many people have been instrumental in the publication of this book, either through their encouragement or direct contact with the material, but three people in particular deserve special recognition. Our grateful thanks go to Peter Newsome, long-time friend and owner of Newsome Travel International in Hong Kong, for his direction, advice, and unfailing assistance at every step of this project. We are greatly indebted as well to Peter Chancellor of Peter Chancellor Design Associates, Hong Kong, for his expertise in the layout, design, graphics, and publication of this book. And we shall always remember and appreciate Mr. Gesang Duoji and his family, of Lhasa, Tibet, for sharing with us the magic of their city.

Copyright © 1987 Christine Johnston Brignoli and Frank J. Brignoli

All rights reserved.
No part of this publication may be reproduced or transmitted in any form or by any means without permission from the publisher.

Published by Peter Chancellor Design Associates, Hong Kong.
A member of The Strongarm Group.
6/F, Yam Tze Commercial Building,
Thomson Road, Hong Kong.

Text by Christine Johnston Brignoli
Photography by Frank J. Brignoli

Creative Focus
Design and print preparation by Peter Chancellor Design Associates.
Printed and bound in Hong Kong by Kadett Printing Co.

> "This centre of Heaven
> This core of the Earth
> This heart of the world
> Fenced round with snow"
> (Anonymous 6th century Tibetan poet)

Kara Tash Dawan
CHONG MUZ TAGH
8920
AKSAI CHIN
Lighten Tso
4898
Jaggitai Tso
Lanak La
5486
Chorol Tso
4724
Kashum Tso
Pangong Tso
C H A N G T A
Rudog
TIBET
ALING KANGRI
7315
Tashigong
Sengge Tsangpo
Gegyai
Gar
Gerze
Tashi Bhug Tso
Sutlej
Tsaparang
Gartok
K A I L A S
7210
5425
Lam La
Sumge
4755
Ngangla Tso
5005
Langchen
Mangk La
KAILAS
6714
N G A R I
Lake Rakas
Mansarowar Lake
Lake
Lang Bu Tso
Coqen
Kyaring Tso
Kagmar
Tangra Tso
5453
Lipu Lekh La
Burang
Paryang
Shoru Tso
Tradum
M
N Y
Raga
Brahmaputra
5645
Saga
Sangsang
Pindu
Tsangpo
Lhatse
DHAULAGIRI
8221
ANNAPURNA
8075
T S A N G
Sakya
A
TIBET
NEPAL
Tingri
Nyalam
EVEREST
200 Km
Kodari
8848
KATHMANDU
KANGCHENJUNGA
A

To Koko Nor Lake
Quinghai (Amdo)
(2 hrs 10m.)
Chumar
Yang Tzu
Flight path
Jinsha Jiang
BASUDAN ULA
Tang La
5180
6096
Dza (Mekong)
(Yang Tzu)
Nyakamor La
(4950)
Sichuan
Amdo
Seling Tso
Amdo Tsonck Tso
Derge
Jomda
Nagqu
Nag (Salween)
Riwoqe
Chamdo
Dzer
4625
Nam Tso
(2hrs 50m)
Flight Path
Dangxung
Sangbagyamda
Baxoi
Rami
Gyamda
Nyingchi
7756
Rawu
Chusul
LHASA
Gyatsa
Gyantse
Gonggar
Tsedang
Yamdrok Tso
Zayu
Pomo Tso
Chayul
Lhuntse
Claimed by China
Cona
THIMPU

Through the centuries, Tibet has been a land of mystery, remote and well hidden behind the imposing icy walls of the Himalayas. Although access to Tibet had always been physically difficult, it was not always forbidden. Over a long and often turbulent time, the country had interacted with India and, more cautiously, with powerful China. In the 17th century, Catholic missionaries were among the first Europeans to cross into Tibet. Even so, very few outsiders succeeded in penetrating Tibet's borders. Fewer still reached the holy city of Lhasa. Faced with incredible natural hardships and imposing dangers, these early adventurers were a hearty breed of explorers, scholars, linguists, eccentrics, spies, and sometimes fugitives, who believed the risks were worth taking.

The political machinations of the 19th century saw tiny Tibet as a potential pawn between the expansionist designs of British India in the south and Imperial Russia far to the north. A protectorate of its huge neighbor China, Tibet was nonetheless aware of its pivotal position on the military gameboard. Fearful of conquest, it sealed its borders, shutting out the world. In spite of this, and at a time when giving aid of any kind to a foreigner within the country meant certain death to a Tibetan, a handful of intrepid and solitary adventurers still managed to reach the remote kingdom. In 1872, Nicholai Przhevalsky, a Russian adventurer, entered Tibet but never reached Lhasa. Nor did William Rockhill, an American diplomat from Peking, in his two attempts shortly afterward. Victory was almost in sight for Annie Royle Taylor, a brave and spirited English missionary, but in 1892 even she was captured, only three days' walk from the holy city. Others were more successful. Wanting to incorporate Tibet into their vast sphere of influence, the British used their military superiority to push an expedition through to Lhasa in 1904 led by Colonel Francis Younghusband. A resultant treaty with the Tibetan government established the position of a British observer and advisor to the Dalai Lama. Sir Charles Bell used his years in this role to develop a sensitive understanding of the Tibetan people and their culture, and became a close friend to the Thirteenth Dalai Lama. Sven Hedin, a famed and enterprising Swedish explorer, travelled Tibet's far-flung regions for ten years without attracting too much attention. Alexandra David-Neel became the first European woman to enter Lhasa. A French Buddhist scholar of renown, she was devoid of any interest in politics, seeking instead religious fulfillment and mystical experiences. In 1923, accompanied by her adopted Tibetan son, Yongden, she disguised herself as a poor beggar and began the hard journey to Lhasa on foot, a journey that would take more than a year. Having previously been ordained by the Panchen Lama in Shigatze, and received in 1910 by the Dalai Lama, in exile at the time in Bhutan, David-Neel had long since acquired the religious credentials to substantiate her position in the Buddhist world. But she was still challenged by what she considered an absurd prohibition against foreigners travelling openly in Tibet, and particularly to Lhasa. A brilliant and courageous eccentric in all ways, she set out for Lhasa to prove that it could be done. Her 1927 book, ***My Journey To Lhasa,*** is one of the most amazing and true travel tales of this century. In 1947, Heinrich Harrer and Peter Aufschneiter, two Austrian mountaineers, escaped their P.O.W. camp in British India and fled into Tibet. Harrer's now-classic ***Seven Years In Tibet,*** relates their hazardous journey and incredible experiences.

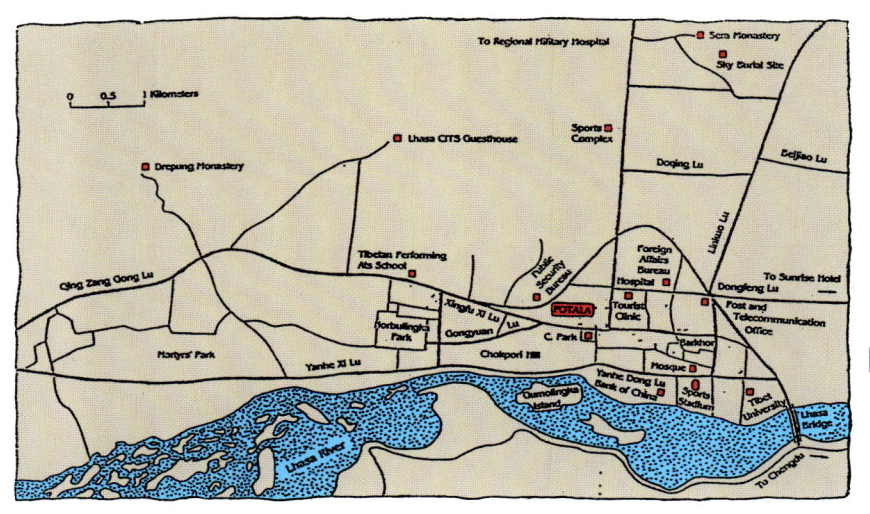

With only fragmentary knowledge of the realities of Tibet, and pitifully incomplete understanding of Buddhist philosophy, legends abounded and fiction was transformed into fact. This mystical mountain realm came to represent a dream place where strange and wonderful things could happen, where huge monasteries hugged rocky cliffs, and where monks could fly through the air. The fascination adventurers had with Tibet grew with every rare scrap of information that occasionally seeped through its borders. Tales were told of wide and barren valleys intersected by silver rivers, strange animals, palaces and gilded temples overflowing with treasure, and the gentle people living in isolation on the "roof of the world." When Songsten Gampo unified Tibet and became its first King more than 13 centuries ago, he introduced Buddhism to the country and created Lhasa as his capital. Its history is filled with years of political upheaval, powerful influence on the rich trade routes through Central Asia, Mongol intrusion by Genghis and Kublai Khan, and tumultuous rivalry between the various sects which evolved in Tibetan Buddhism. The great Fifth and Thirteenth Dalai Lamas proved themselves enlightened leaders of their people, but for over a thousand years there were few advancements. Life remained basically feudal in nature, relieved only by the religious fervour of the people.

And so it was for hundreds of years until September 9, 1951 when the Peoples' Liberation Army entered Lhasa and the government of China absorbed this independent monarchy. In 1979, the Chinese government cautiously opened a door on Tibet, allowing a few visitors to enter. Just a trickle at first, the ground swell of interest is becoming a flood. Today, while still not easy to reach Lhasa, it is possible. With relaxed regulations and a choice of routes, travellers can make the journey by air or overland from China or Nepal. The mystique of Tibet is clearly very much alive.

From Chengdu in the Szechuan province of China, the flight to Lhasa is a mere two hours of mountain skipping over some of the world's tallest peaks, and smooth gliding over the barren and desolate purple-shaded hills of Tibet. Gleaming ribbons of rivers brighten the vegetation-less landscape, and solitary wanderers miles from anywhere hang prayer flags on whatever bit of tree or rock they pass. This is Tibet, land of oxygen-thin air, impossibly blue skies, and the great monasteries which once fed this mountain theocracy. An undeniable magic exist about the place. Any admirer of those brave early adventurers could not help but feel a rush of excitement and yet a stab of sorrow that Time and the vagaries of world politics have altered the visions today's travellers will see.

Lhasa, in its lofty perch at 12,000 feet, is yet another 80 kilometer journey from the airport at Gonggar. Following the Yarlong Tsampo and Quxu Rivers, few settlements exist along this spectacular way. Rounding a last curve in the road, the golden rooftops of the fabulous Potala Palace gleam in the distance. In the traditional Tibetan view of things, Lhasa was long believed to be the centre of the universe. The small city lays neatly nestled on a plain, protected by what at 16,000 feet would not be called 'hills' anywhere else in the world.

A holy city, Lhasa was the home of some of Tibet's most sacred shrines and a popular destination for pilgrims coming from outlying areas. Punctuated at varying points by elaborate and periodically guarded gates, the Lingkhor was the famous ring-road which encircled the city. Alongside this road, Tibetans often set up camps, complete with comfortable tents appliqued with brightly colored Buddhist symbols. Here, in an atmosphere of festivity, they would enjoy picnics and outings, greet friends or relatives returning from journeys, or bid them safe travel as they set off. The rich and poor trod this road together for centuries.

Aristocratic officials dressed in brocades and fur passed this way, as did their wives in coral and turquoise encrusted headdresses. Nomads from the north, pilgrims, squalid beggars, and incarnate lamas, all would enter the holy city from the Lingkhor. In the wake of new Chinese construction, the Lingkhor has all but vanished, replaced by a thoroughly unimaginative asphalt road. Thus, one's vision of this important part of Lhasa must be left to old photographs, accounts by some of those early travellers, or the imagination.

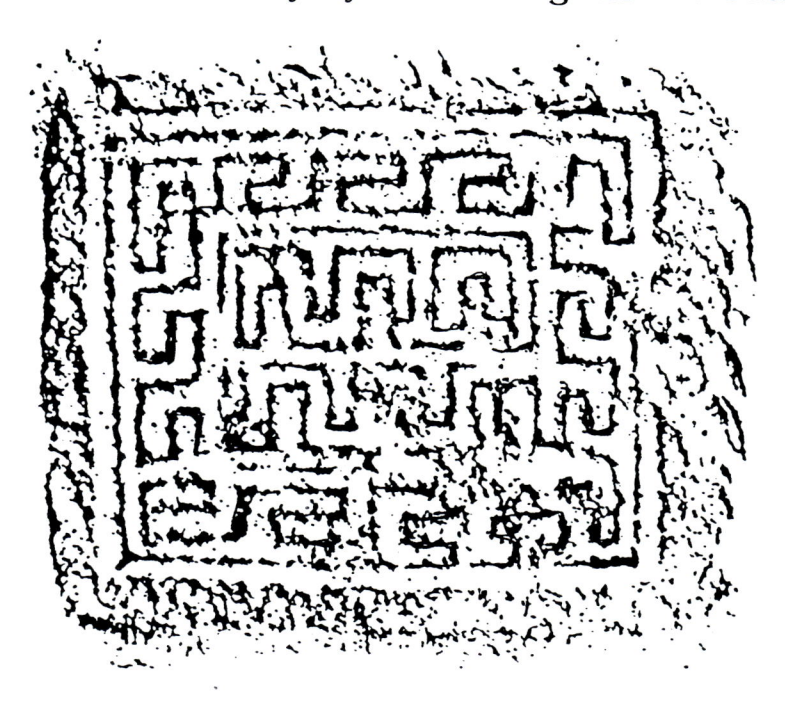

Happily, a similar and perhaps even more important circular road in Old Lhasa still remains. The Barkhor surrounds the Jokhang Temple, Lhasa's most revered holy place, the spiritual heart of all Tibet. Hundreds of Tibetans circumnavigate this timeless route daily, clock-wise in Buddhist fashion. Many have come long distances to spin their prayer wheels or make their devotional progress by body lengths along the dusty ground, reciting sutras as they go. Fragrant smoke billows from large incense burners, and people meet each other with the traditional Tibetan greeting, simultaneously sticking out their tongue and smiling. The Barkhor, Lhasa's market-place, teems with cheerful, red-cheeked Tibetans selling their incredible wares. Small stalls offer prayer flags in colors to denote the sky, clouds, fire, water, and earth. Prayer wheels, those magical cylinders of copper, brass and wood, are filled with printed prayers to be sent Heaven-bound with each rotation. Shoppers purchase "khatas," finely woven white silk scarves, to present as signs of respect. Every booth offers something of wonder, a visual feast of the strange and fascinating fruits of Tibetan culture. Here one finds prayer beads and amulet cases, tinder boxes and silver encased conch shells. Copper and brass monastic trumpets, butter churns and lamps are spread out for display as are carpets, fur hats, and stacks of hand-painted prayers on rough paper. The solitary pelt of a snow leopard hangs against a wall. The people are welcoming and smiles light their wrinkled sunburned faces. Most wear traditional clothing and the Barkhor is a swirl of sheepskin coats worn off one arm by many of the men, and women in long, dark dresses relieved by colorful aprons. In a scene hardly changed from that viewed by Genghis Khan, the Barkhor is Tibet in miniature. A red-robed monk peers through ancient purple spectacles intricately hinged with silver. A dwarf beggar crouches over her bowl of alms. Khampas from eastern Tibet stroll the area in furry robes and bright red headdresses, daggers hanging from their belts. Incense merchants spread their aromatic shrubs and juniper branches on bits of cloth along the road. But for the jarring presence of modern cassette tapes, and

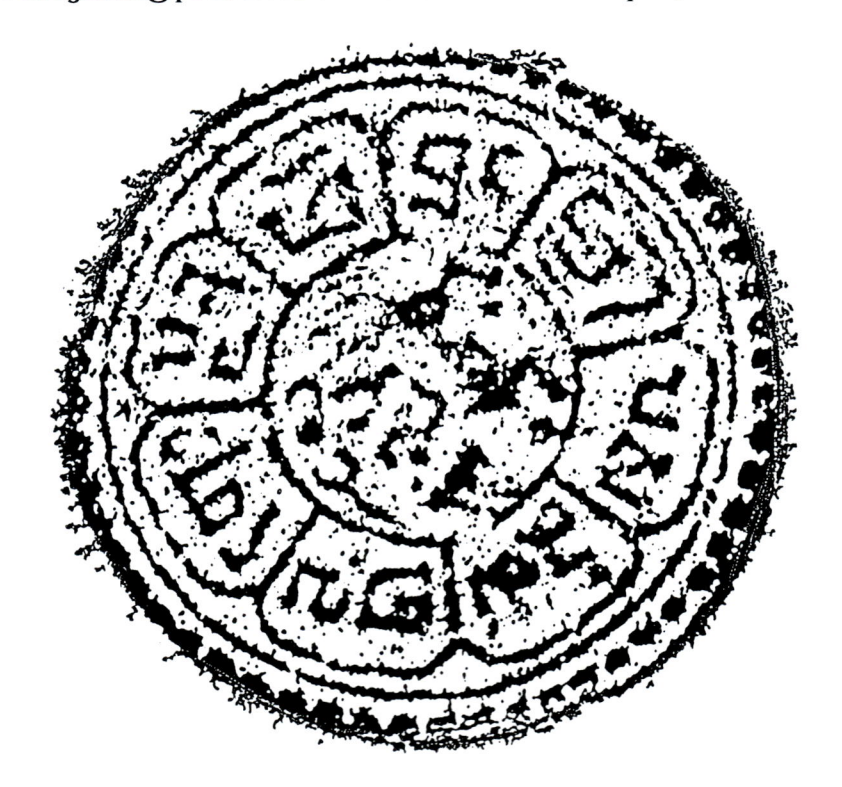

To Tibetans, the Dalai Lama has always been the most revered personage of spiritual and temporal power. Welcomed as the incarnation of Chenrezi, the Buddha of Compassion, he is not selected but discovered by a complicated means of prophetic guidance. Before his death in 1933, the Thirteenth Dalai Lama had given signs of his coming re-birth. Guided by visions seen in Lhamoi Latso, the Sacred Lake, and prophesies uttered by the State Oracle, a group of high lamas journeyed to Eastern Tibet in 1939. There, in the small village of Taktser, they discovered a young child, son of a poor farmer. The lamas charged with this all-important task had known the previous Dalai Lama well. They carried with them some of his personal belongings, as well as imitations intended to confuse all but the real successor.

Convinced of his authenticity after a series of tests, they began plans for the long and difficult journey which would bring this child to Lhasa with his family. The trip took several months, each stage marked by jubilant celebrations. For the Tibetan people, the knowledge of a new Dalai Lama in their midst, on whom they could depend for wisdom and guidance,

garishly colored plastics offered in some booths, it is an intriguing time-warp. Like spokes of a wheel, narrow streets extend off the Barkhor. Houses of two-storied traditional design crowd this part of the town. The Ahetsangu Nunnery, a place of retreat for Buddhist women, is close by. Tibetans sometimes approach visitors on the Barkhor to quietly ask for pictures of the Fourteenth Dalai Lama, their god-king who remains in exile in Dharamsala, India. Even after three decades of Chinese rule, the strength of their religion remains the focus of life for the majority of Tibetans as it has for over a thousand years.

was reason for great rejoicing. When he fled Tibet in 1959 to set up his government in exile in India, thousands of Tibetans followed, but for those who remain, the influence of the Dalai Lama is still great.

Before the introduction of Buddhism to Tibet, the people followed an ancient animistic religion called Bon. This fearful mixture of magic, sacrifice, and terrifying gods had enveloped the Tibetan people for centuries. But to the south, between India and Nepal, the preachings of an ascetic named Guatama had begun to revolutionize religious thinking. Called the Buddha – "The Enlightened One" – by his followers, he taught the simple yet demanding principles which became both an intricate philosophical and metaphysical system and one of the world's great religions. However, another thousand years were to pass before these teachings began to take root in Tibet and probably, at first, only as symbols of an even more powerful magic than that offered by Bon. Tradition holds that Songsten Gampo, the unifier of Tibet, helped solidify the creation of his new kingdom in the 7th century A.D. by the introduction of Buddhism, to which he himself may have been converted by his Nepalese and Chinese wives. To the primitive existence of Tibet's pre-history, Buddhism brought centuries of architecture, painting, sculpture, music, reading and writing – in short, civilization.

But Buddhism offered something even greater than all the outward trappings of culture. It offered a spiritual message of such attractiveness that Tibetan conversion was soon universal. Buddha preached four noble truths: that misery is part and parcel of human existence, that misery originates from desire, that desire can be eliminated and that, by following a virtuous path, desire—and therefore suffering—can be completely overcome. These virtuous actions in thought, word, and deed were soon woven into a moral code which became the cement of life in Tibet, as it already had in other parts of Asia. The taking of any life, human or animal, was forbidden, as were stealing, lying and any impure actions. The religion strongly encouraged kindness, love, and peacefulness. In Buddhism, spiritual progress takes place over many successive reincarnations. These are affected by the laws of karma, the commission and resulting consequence of good or bad deeds. Meditation on the

A rubbing from an intricately carved wood block used to print Tibetan prayer flags.

various stages of spiritual life and their inextricable relationship to goodness became a central pillar of belief. Through a conscious effort to live a moral and, as far as possible, enlightened existence, Buddhism offered each Tibetan the chance to improve his lot in his next life. Developing the human intellect in ways both wise and worthy became a personal responsibility, and one taken seriously, particularly with the advent of the great monasteries, those bastions of religious teaching throughout Tibet. As Buddhism spread, its influence as a religion became indistinguishable from its influence as a lifestyle. The two were irrevokably linked. Tibet was nothing if not religion. With the introduction of Buddhism — although centuries of evolution of a distinctive style lay ahead — Tibet had moved out of the darkness and into the light.

Dating from the time of King Songsten Gampo, the Jokhang Temple is one of the spectacular sites of Old Lhasa, and the magnet which draws Tibetan pilgrims at least once in their lifetime. It was built to house what Tibetans consider the most sacred image of Buddha. The presence of this figure of Buddha has always imparted a special holiness to the city of Lhasa. Believed to have been brought from China by Princess Wen Cheng, one of the King's two wives, turquoise and jewels encrust this gilded statue, the greatest of all national treasures. Behind a screen of metal chains, its immense significance protected it even during the tumultuous upheaval of the Cultural Revolution, which damaged or destroyed many of Tibet's religious shrines.

Despite the dark and somewhat other-worldly appearance of the interior of the Jokhang, the rich splendors of Tibetan art are evident inside the multitude of chapels and communal prayer areas. The light of butter lamps illuminates intricate wall paintings and the place seems alive with statues of deities, and ferocious demons. These demons, often with multiple heads or arms, are probably remnants of Bon, Tibet's primitive religion, carried over into Buddhism in the role of protectors. Beautiful "thangkas," or religious paintings on cloth, decorate the multitude of shrines in the Jokhang, as do carved wooden columns.

Though the interior of the temple has a haunting and shadowy quality about it, the rooftop is magnificent for its brilliance of color and sunlight. Gilded pagoda-style roofs gleam against Tibet's incredible blue sky, and golden religious symbols crown the corners of each wall. Temple bells with metal prayers as clappers are suspended from wooden eaves and ring quietly in the breeze, while dragon-like griffons perch in protective stance. Numerous buildings and workshops fill the rooftop. Here master artists sit cross-legged, patiently painting statues of Buddha. From the roof of the Jokhang, the near-by Potala Palace looms large atop its own hill, and the great monasteries of Sera and Drepung are not far away.

While temples like the Jokhang were special places of worship, the monasteries were the religious communities which served them, and the sites of Tibet's famed theological institutions. Not only the physical heart of Tibetan culture and religion, the monasteries were important pillars of the government as well. Every Tibetan family was expected to give up at least one son to the monkhood, and did so with little resistance. By becoming a monk, that son lightened his family's economic burden by moving into a monastery which provided for his needs. By educational achievement he would bring great honor to his family and perhaps become a revered lama. Only a few kilometers west of Lhasa, Drepung Monastery, once Tibet's largest and richest, sits built up against holy Mt. Gyengbuwudze. A vast city in itself, Drepung was founded in 1416. It once housed as many as 10,000 monks, though only a few hundred remain today. As with all monasteries not completely destroyed in the Chinese "acculturation of Tibet," Drepung is a treasure house of Buddhist art and wisdom. For the more than five centuries of their great influence, monasteries grouped monks in sections according to their geographical origins and dialects. A high lama presided over each and was responsible for delegating the day to day duties required for the smooth operation of his particular college. As well as covering the varied aspects of teaching, housing and feeding the monks under his control, this lama managed properties, administrative and financial affairs, and maintained order and discipline. The abbot, the highest ranking monastic official, sat at the very top of the chain of power and authority. Ultimately accountable for everything that happened at the monastery, he was also directly involved in certain decisions taken by the government.

Young aristocratic children sometimes received secular education if their parents could afford the fees of a famed Rinpoche, or learned lama, to teach the intricacies of Sanskrit and mathematics. But the great monasteries were the only major centres of religious learning in pre-1951 Tibet. Though these monasteries had been established primarily to educate, talent is never equally distributed. Inevitably, a pyramid-shaped arrangement of human resources evolved, with those at each level providing something for the general good.

The comparatively few monks at the top had proven themselves scholarly enough to pursue the rigorous program of dialectics, doctrine, sacred liturgy, and the intricacies of Buddhist thought. It often took a fine scholar-monk over twenty years of concerted study to complete his basic courses and then move on to still higher levels of enlightenment. Obviously, those who entered monastic programs with a solid background of secular education enjoyed an advantage from the beginning. Other intellectual monks chose to specialize in traditional medicine or astronomy, both highly regarded disciplines which required aptitude and serious study.

A future in the hierarchy of the monastery, and perhaps the government, was assured to those who passed difficult examinations proving their mastery of theology, medicine, and astronomy. Each monastery also had a very talented and specialized group of artists. These unknown masters contributed to the beauty of their surroundings through their complex religious art. Using the medium of wall paintings, sculpture, silken hangings, wood carvings, thangkas, metal castings of images of Buddha, even embroidery of the eight auspicious religious symbols, this segment of the monastic population produced much of the Tibetan art still appreciated today. Other monks were trained primarily to deal with the simple religious needs of the general public. They performed the rites to bring good luck or keep evil powers at bay, told fortunes, or ministered to the sick and dying. But, the vast majority of monks in any monastery were quite ordinary indeed, the worker-bees of communal life. With no particularly outstanding talents, they were the manual labourers, the kitchen workers, clerks, builders, discipline enforcers, and the maintenance men on whom the operation of these vast cities depended. A lifetime of serving others in the monastery was no doubt a small price to pay for food, shelter, companionship and minimal education. For most, it was the only means of escaping certain poverty.

The Wheel of Dharma
Also called the Wheel of Law, the Wheel of Dharma represents the Sakyamuni Buddha himself, and the relationship of all things.

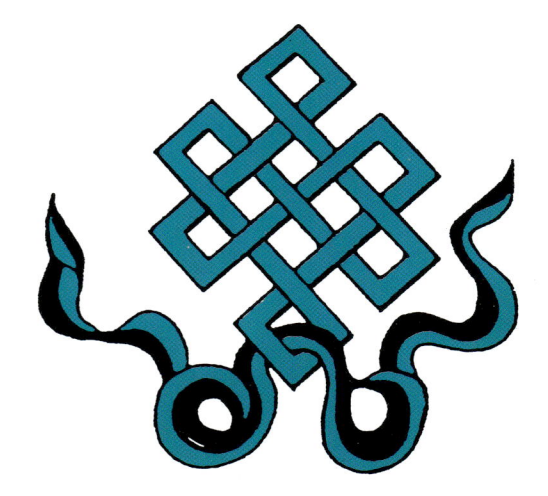

The Eternal Knot
The eternal knot is symbolic of the unity of all things. Often found appliqued on fabric monastic awnings, the eternal knot is also a common feature in religious art.

The Two Fish
Always shown in a swimming position, the two fish represent the spiritual liberation granted by Buddhism.

The Conch Shell
Scientific evidence has shown that hundreds of millions of years ago the Tibetan plateau was on the bottom of the sea. Fossils of underwater life continue to be found throughout Tibet. Conch shells have come to represent the spoken word, and are often used as vessels containing butter, or as trumpets in Buddhist worship.

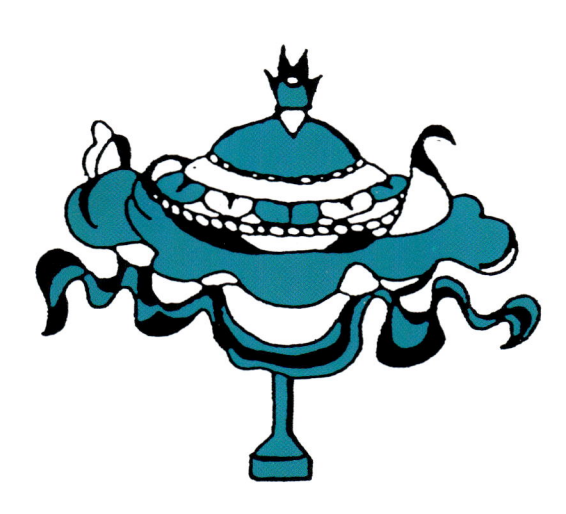

The Parasol
Shown with streamers, the parasol is a sign of royalty.

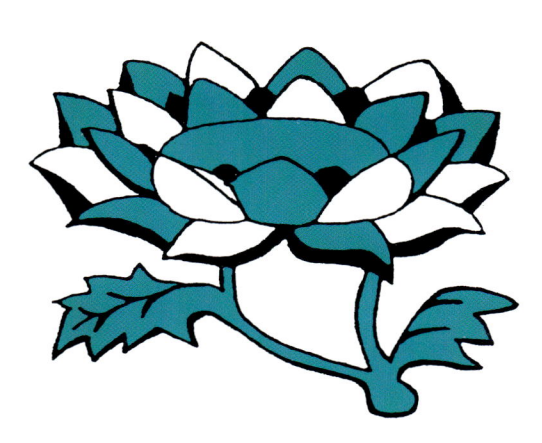

The Lotus
The lotus is a common Buddhist symbol. Rising in beauty from very ordinary roots, it is believed to represent nirvana, that perfect state of being, which grows from the squalid existence of this world.

The Banner of Victory
Cylindrical in shape, whether of fabric or metal, the Banner of Victory is symbolic of victory over ignorance and death.

The Wish-Fulfilling Vase
In various forms, the wish-fulfilling vase appears often in Buddhist art, sometimes as gilded finials on temple rooftops. It is believed to be a sacred urn, symbolic of hidden treasure.

Drepung is an ancient complex built in ascending fashion against the mountainside. Stone pathways or steps link each of the many buildings. Red-robed monks come and go while stray dogs in countless numbers sleep in the sunshine. Plain and once whitewashed, the dormitory buildings with their open windows are grimy and dark with age. Each monk has a tiny cell in which he lives, sleeps and meditates. The sacred buildings, topped with golden objects, as the "Wheel of Dharma" held between resting deer, have interiors painted in bright colors. Extraordinary murals relieve the darkness of these old buildings lit primarily by butter votive lamps. Every wall displays intricate and ancient paintings of deities, demons, and the Tibetan view of the realms of existence. Statues of the various Dalai Lamas abound, some tiny, some huge, all gilded. Pillars divide the halls hung with beautiful thangkas. Butter lamps are everywhere, constantly replenished by the donations of pilgrims who come in never-ending lines. Melted butter in a conch shell is sometimes poured into their hands or upon their heads by a monk. Prayer wheels, individually hand-held or enormous mounted ones spun as you walk by, are always in motion. In the main chanting hall, rows and rows of monks, red-robed and of all ages, sit quietly on long mats while the abbot delivers a sermon, perhaps chastizing them for going to Lhasa to drink 'chang,' barley wine.

The kitchens at Drepung seem like a scene straight from "The Sorcerer's Apprentice." In these dark, medieval rooms butter in large black kettles slowly melts over a smoking fire. Monks scurry about ladling butter enriched tea into wooden pitchers so it can be taken at a run, still steaming, into the chanting halls. Pilgrims come to these kitchens to make their donation to the monastery: a great block of butter, a sack of barley meal, or a brick of Indian or Chinese tea. In so harsh and barren a part of the world, Tibetans long ago adapted themselves to a simple diet of 'tsampa,' roast barley flour mixed with butter and tea into a paste. Cakes made of cheese, butter and sugar; and salted butter tea make up the remainder of the diet. None of these ingredients contradicts the strong Buddhist admonition against the taking of any life. Stemming from their unshakeable belief in reincarnation, meat and fish were traditionally consumed only in times of extreme emergencies, and always with an accompanying prayer begging forgiveness.

The sacred chanting halls of the monastery are dark and pillared places hung with intricate silken banners worn by centuries of religious fervor. The paintings come to life in the flicker of the lamps. "Khatas" drape many statues. These white silk scarves used often in Tibetan society are presented to pay homage to figures of Buddha. They are also given on the occasion of weddings, births and funerals, or to bid farewell to an honored person about to leave on a journey.

In quiet corners, small groups of monks form 'torma,' holy food, which is placed before the countless gilded deities. Pilgrims come here, young and old, all devout. Women and men carry prayer beads and quietly utter sutras. Some prostrate themselves before statues, or move along the floor by body lengths. Even today, the majority of Tibetans remain devout Buddhists.

Ancient ladders, their railings slick with the butter-coated grasp of hands over Time, lead the way to the Drepung rooftops. The Lhasa valley spreads itself below. This serene place, silent and beautiful, spills across to the river, hills, and mountains beyond. The clear air and brilliance of light at 12,000 feet transform this view into a surreal and enormous picture. Outside the labryinth of Drepung, smoke from carefully tended incense fires almost obscures huge rock paintings. Beyond are walls of prayer stones, rocks which bear the universal mantra "Om mani padme hum" inscribed in Tibetan characters. These devoutly created mani stones represent prayers offered by pilgrims. Colorful prayer flags flutter from nearby trees or bushes.

The small monastery of Nechung sits at the foot of the Drepung road. The powerful Chief State Oracle, an important figure in the old government of Tibet, once made his home here. Chosen for spiritual purity, the better to contact good rather than evil forces, this monk would regularly go into a hypnotic trance, gesticulate, dance about and speak in intriguing riddles. The government avidly consulted the Oracle for his prophesies and advice. The last official Oracle advised the young Fourteenth Dalai Lama until 1959 when Tibet's leader fled to exile in India.

Founded in 1419, Lhasa's other premier monastery, Sera, is also more than 500 years old. Although continually eclipsed by Drepung's great governmental influence, Sera was once a significant rival, both in physical size and number of monks in residence. Sera's hierarchy included many powerful lamas whose political protection assured its position as a monastery of major importance. Always aware of the serious and sometimes volatile competition and political intrigue between the two monasteries, an infamous army of monk soldiers was created at Sera. Called "dob-dobs," their intimidating ferocity and zealous single-mindedness were renowned long before early western explorers described them. As late as 1950 the "dob-dobs" were a force to be reckoned with. Sera nestles at the base of Tatipu Hill on the northern edge of Lhasa.

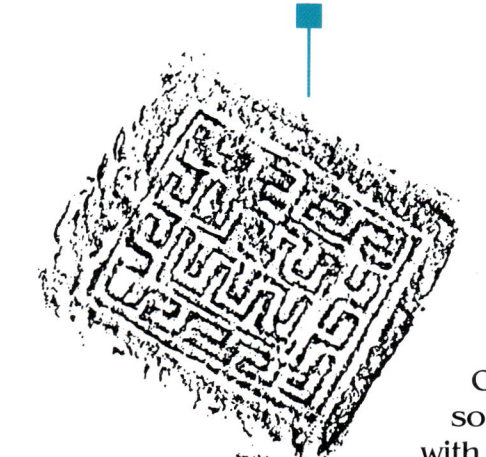

The monastery sprawls and has wider avenues between buildings and fewer steps to climb from one level to another than at Drepung. But in all other ways, the ancient monastic architecture remains virtually the same. Now begrimed with age, sloping stone walls are a traditional feature of Tibetan religious buildings. In a uniquely Tibetan style of sacred decoration, the upper exterior walls of the holiest buildings are covered with thousands of twigs packed tightly together and painted a reddish-brown color. In wide courtyards, prayer flags flutter from tall poles, made of narrow tree trunks carefully fitted together. The hanging of prayer flags, for Tibetans, seems almost a universal sign of religious devotion. Whenever possible, they are raised on these towering staves. Those who could afford the expense always erected a prayer pole on the rooftop of their house, or in the garden. For others, any bit of tree or shrub would do. These colorful and symbolic entreaties constantly remind us of the fervour of Tibetan Buddhists.

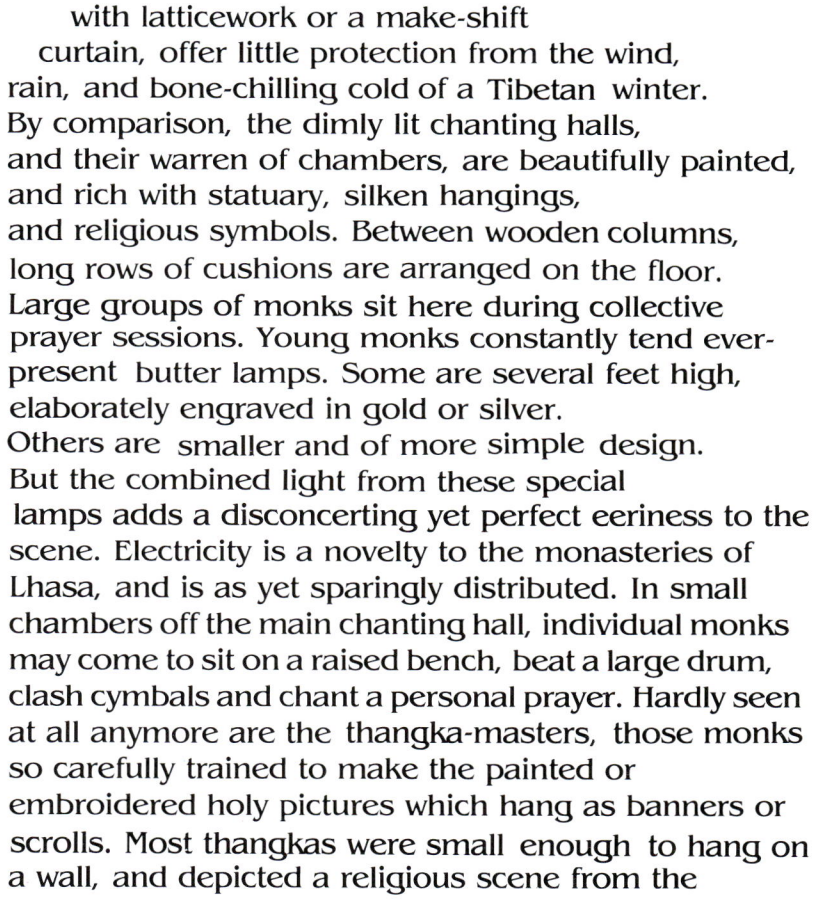

The dormitories at Sera, as in all other monasteries, are spartan and squalid places for the few hundred monks who remain. Open windows, some covered only with latticework or a make-shift curtain, offer little protection from the wind, rain, and bone-chilling cold of a Tibetan winter. By comparison, the dimly lit chanting halls, and their warren of chambers, are beautifully painted, and rich with statuary, silken hangings, and religious symbols. Between wooden columns, long rows of cushions are arranged on the floor. Large groups of monks sit here during collective prayer sessions. Young monks constantly tend ever-present butter lamps. Some are several feet high, elaborately engraved in gold or silver. Others are smaller and of more simple design. But the combined light from these special lamps adds a disconcerting yet perfect eeriness to the scene. Electricity is a novelty to the monasteries of Lhasa, and is as yet sparingly distributed. In small chambers off the main chanting hall, individual monks may come to sit on a raised bench, beat a large drum, clash cymbals and chant a personal prayer. Hardly seen at all anymore are the thangka-masters, those monks so carefully trained to make the painted or embroidered holy pictures which hang as banners or scrolls. Most thangkas were small enough to hang on a wall, and depicted a religious scene from the boundless symbolism of Tibetan religion. But each of Tibet's greatest monasteries once owned enormous thangkas which, when hung from the roof-level on ceremonial days, would cascade several stories to the ground in what must have been an awesome display of beauty and spiritual significance to the throngs below. Today, pilgrims still make their way to Sera Monastery, as they do to any of the sacred shrines remaining in the country. While Chinese roads and buses now traverse some of Tibet's wilderness, many pilgrims may, by choice or necessity, have walked for days or weeks to reach these places of devotion. Watching them is sometimes every bit as fascinating as seeing the shrines themselves. Whether dressed in modern clothing or wrapped in the rough sheepskins of nomads from the north, they come in constant streams, a living testimony of the failure of politics to extinguish the flames of their devout religious belief. They understand the relative unimportance of this temporary earthly existence.

Priceless Buddhist scriptures known as "sungten" rest in the libraries of Tibet's great monasteries. As well as being significant from a literary or theological point of view, each book is a masterpiece of Buddhist art. The Tibetan written language developed in about the 7th century A.D. as an offshoot of Sanskrit. For hundreds of years, these books were hand-inscribed on long, narrow sheets of rough Tibetan paper. A monk then stacked the individual sheets between wooden or more elaborate covers, and protected them with layers of silken wrappings. As in medieval Europe, scribes in a multitude of Tibetan monasteries painstakingly copied and illustrated these religious works. This accumulation of sacred texts formed the basis of impressive libraries. While many of these early calligraphers wrote with a simple solution of ash, others created letters of gold, silver, copper, iron, and cinnabar. A set of the 108 volume Kangyur scriptures was routinely commissioned for each of the more important monasteries. The script was entirely hand-written in precious metals. Six centuries later, block printing methods were sophisticated enough to make the mass-production of these books possible. The Buddhist Scripture Printing House, at the base of the Potala Palace, was one of the most important publishing centres in Tibet. Although the Cultural Revolution destroyed many of these priceless works, countless others have survived. They are stacked floor to ceiling high, sometimes behind protective screens of wire mesh. Only a few people can decipher them any longer. Over the centuries, the spoken Tibetan language deviated continually from the original written language. The introduction of Chinese in 1951 has further muddied the waters and now the continuity of this treasure trove of Tibetan ecclesiastical thought is quickly disappearing.

From the gilded rooftops of Sera Monastery, birds of carrion circle and dive toward the place of "celestial burial" on the other side of the mountain. Funeral practices varied widely in Tibet, based on ethnic group, geographic location, and financial or social status. In the past, the very poor placed the bodies of their dead into the rivers. Burial in the ground was generally reserved for those who died of infectious diseases or had committed serious crimes. Cremation was chosen only for learned scholars, whose ashes were scattered on the winds. Exceptionally exalted persons as Dalai Lamas or Panchen Lamas were entombed inside a stupa or chorten. But the majority of Tibetans over the centuries chose celestial burial, and do to this day. Although a ritual alien to the West, it remains very pragmatic and meaningful in Tibet. After a period of several days of mourning, bearers take the body to a special and deserted area. Here, on a large rock outcrop, an undertaker dismembers it, cutting the flesh into small pieces and setting them to one side. The bones are carefully ground to powder, mixed with tsampa, and fed to the vultures which hover over this lonely place. They then consume the flesh. All traces of the body must be disposed of before the soul can leave on its search for a new home. Understandably, vultures are deemed sacred birds in Tibet for the important part they play in celestial burial. Reincarnation is a central tenet of Buddhism. As such, the actual method of disposing of a body is insignificant. In celestial burial, the symbolism of the soul soaring through the air as it reaches its next existence is appealing.

For the majority of Tibetans who live in inaccessible parts of the wilderness of this country, the yak is the mainstay of life. This powerful and shaggy creature is rarely seen elsewhere in the world. A high altitude beast of burden it can carry huge loads over difficult terrain, even in the coldest of weather. Though the most devout Tibetans rarely eat meat, milk from these animals makes the butter needed for existence here. When Western writers continually refer to this butter as 'yak butter', Tibetans are amused, for in their language only the male of the species is called a 'yak.' Butter is made from the thick, rich milk of the female, a 'dri.' Whatever gender,

Symbolic of wisdom, the "dorje" or thunderbolt is a ritual object in Tibetan Buddhism.

the skins are used in a multitude of ways including clothing and thick-soled boots. Coracles or small, light-weight boats, were a traditional means of transport for Tibetans who lived close to rivers. In this ancient and primitive design, yak skins covered a sturdy framework of willow, and the boatman would use a paddle to direct his small craft. Ponies and horses accompanying journeyers would swim alongside, their reins held from inside the boat. Heinrich Harrer describes his sorrowful 1950 departure from Tibet as beginning with just such a voyage, down the Kyichu River to its junction with the mighty Brahmaputra. Today, a few small coracles can still be seen swirling on the fast currents of the Kyichu River which runs through Lhasa.

The Norbulingka was built as a royal summer palace by the Seventh Dalai Lama in 1755. Only a few kilometers from the Potala Palace, this one hundred acres of grass, trees, and flowers provided a bright and refreshing contrast to the enormity of the somber Potala.

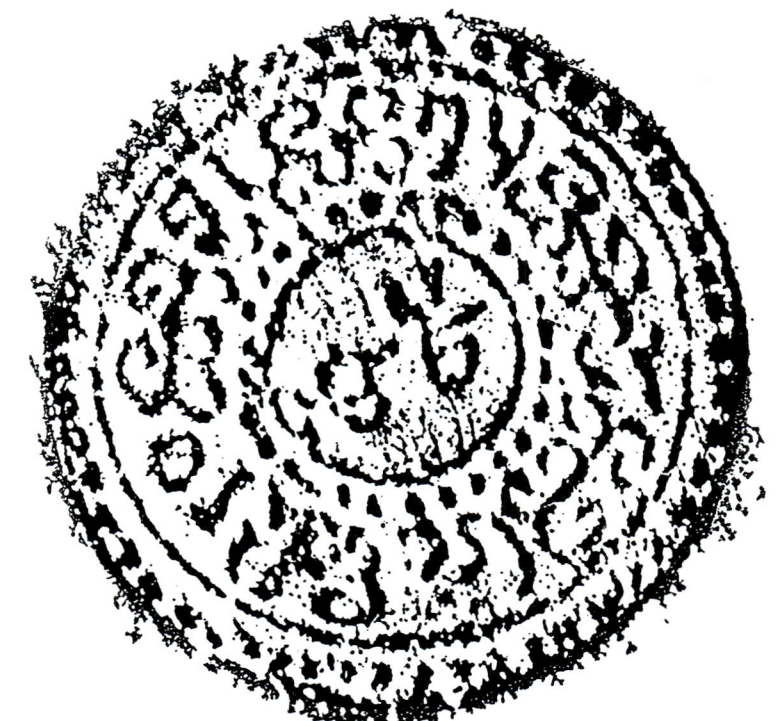

Each spring, in a grand and colorful procession, the king and his court wound their way through Lhasa toward the comfort of their summer quarters. Behind the yellow walls of the Norbulingka lie the remnants of a private zoo and several palaces, including the one built for the Fourteenth Dalai Lama shortly before he fled to India. In the "Jewelled Garden," a special private enclosure for the enjoyment of the Dalai Lama, Heinrich Harrer tutored his young charge, amazed at his natural engineering talents and interest in films and books from abroad. Like any other royal residence, entrance to the Norbulingka was forbidden to all but the very few, and access to the God-King's home was especially rare. Today, Tibetans come in droves to stand in silent, reverent lines, or prostrate themselves before this place, now considered a shrine. All has been kept inside as it was that night in 1959 when the Dalai Lama made his successful escape on horseback. Caretakers wearing sheepwool slippers skate their way across wooden floors in the palace, dusting and polishing as they go. Complex religious murals cover the walls but the furnishings are sparse and simple. The king's radio, record player, and collection of favorite recordings remain in his study, as does a small porcelain cup on a table, refilled each day in hopeful anticipation of his return. Silk khatas hang from photographs of the Dalai Lama, his royal throne, even from the mouths of the white stone lions which guard the Norbulingka, giving them silly smiles and diaphanous whiskers. In a country where modern sanitation is still a novelty, the gleaming tile and stainless steel bathroom in the palace is revolutionary. In the Tibet of of the 1950's, it must have been even more confounding. Foreign luxuries were uncommon in Tibet. Those few which were imported, even the Dalai Lama's yellow motorcar, had to be carried in pieces on the backs of porters across the Himalayas from India.

Lhasa's jewel in the crown, the Potala Palace, dominates the city from its lofty position atop Red Hill. As the symbol of Tibet it is its most famous sight. Thirteen stories high, with over a thousand rooms, it is a world in itself. The Potala was not only the residence of the Dalai Lama, but the center of religious and political power in the Tibetan government. While a fortress-palace existed on this hill for over a thousand years, the present Potala itself is more than three centuries old. It has survived Time, several severe earthquakes, and the destruction caused by the Cultural Revolution. In its enormity, it is clothed in steep whitewashed walls and is crowned with the magnificent golden rooftops which could be seen from miles away by pilgrims as they approached the holy city. The massive Potala must surely be one of the architectural wonders of the world. The top sections are divided in two parts. The Red Palace, so-called because of its traditional reddish architecture, was the seat of religious power. It contained the living quarters of high officials, great libraries, beautiful temples and shrines, as well as the tombs of former Dalai Lamas. The White Palace was the seat of government and residence of the god-king. His private apartments at the very top of the Potala were close and confining. The Fourteenth Dalai Lama, a young boy-king, relieved his sense of isolation by wistfully watching his subjects below through a telescope mounted on the roof. Connecting these two palaces is a small yellow building which houses the giant thangkas, those banners hung from the top of the palace on special religious occasions. The eight sacred symbols of Buddhism appear everywhere, the parasol, the two fish, the conch shell, the eternal knot, the banner of victory, the Wheel of Dharma, the lotus, and the wish-fulfilling vase. A warren of tiny chambers weave through the dark recesses of the palace. Here were the once-rich treasuries of the Dalai Lama and the State, narrow monastic cells, the kitchens and the dungeons. At the foot of the Potala, in the district called Sho, was once the famed printing house which produced many of the religious publications of Tibet.

Heavy wooden doors of the Potala open onto a dark, medieval world enveloped in perpetual religious art. Every chamber is covered with paintings, thangkas, statues of benign deities, and their demonic protectors, with the light from butter lamps casting a wierd glow over all. Climbing up and down ladders to reach the different levels of the palace, the sound of chanting monks and the cacophony of eerie music carries on the wind. On yet another rooftop under gilded eaves and golden finials sparkling against the sky, sit fourteen

monks, in two rows, facing each other. Dressed in their
garnet robes, and with closely cropped heads,
they chant in unison to the accompaniment of their
holy music, the dull thumping of a skin drum,
the clash of cymbals, tinkle of bells, and the strange
piercing sound emanating from a long copper horn.
In a ritual as timeless as Tibet itself, only the occasional
flash of a Chinese wristwatch today adds
an odd counterpoint to the scene.

Through the palace, hallways are hung with giant
drums and medieval weapons, coats of Tibetan-style
chain-mail and other wonders of past centuries. All are
blackened by the touch of
hands over time. Ahead is
the great staircase,
almost as famous as
the Potala itself.
Uneven and steep,
it zig-zags back
and forth as
it winds its way
to the bottom.

Chokpori, the near-by Medicine King Hill, was once
one of four holy mountains of Tibet. Over three
hundred years ago, a famous school of traditional
medicine was founded here. Pilgrim footpaths wound
their way up the hillside, and prayer flags and stones
decorated each turn. Heavily bombarded during the
1959 uprisings, the medical school was destroyed and
a powerful antenna now tops the hill.

The fascination of Tibet is seductive, the
mysteriousness of its ways only compounded
by the gentleness of its people. Whatever the
destiny of this tiny country, its rich cultural and religious
heritage lives on in the minds and memories of those who
have come to see it and those who have only read of its
wonders. In a frantic and often confused world, it might
seem just as easy to forget the people of this remote
and snow-clad nation whose dearest wish was to live in
peace and freedom. Yet, they shall be remembered,
for in the words of Heinrich Harrer, Tibet is "a dream
mankind wanted to dream…"

Potala Palace

Reflected in the waters of a nearby lake, the immense Potala Palace is the symbol of Tibet and a wonder of architectural genius.

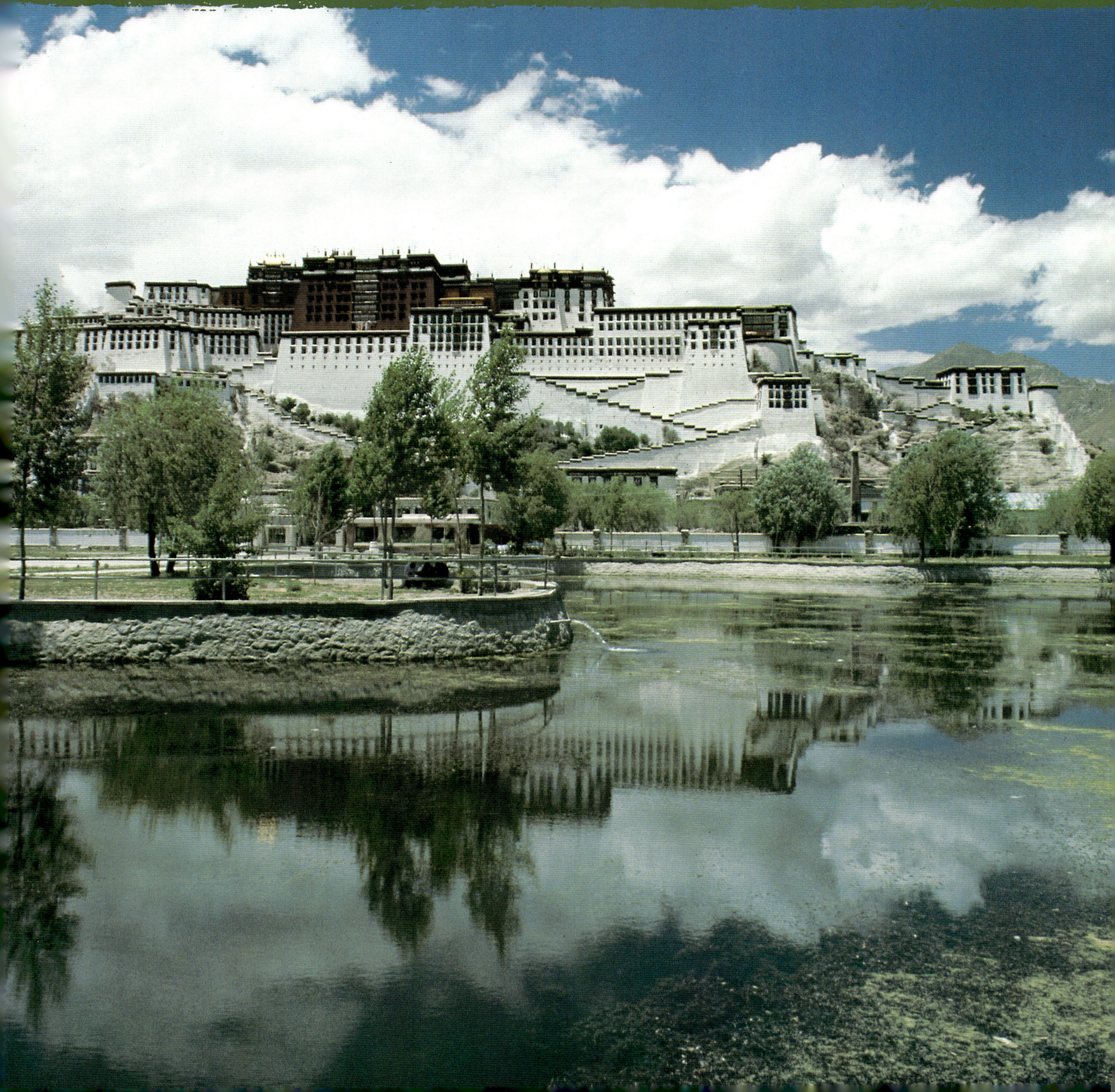

From the north, the Potala palace dominates the city of Lhasa, protected by rugged mountain guardians.

Descending the famous southern staircase, the nearby Chokpori Hill is visible. Once the site of a renown school of Tibetan traditional medicine, it is topped now by a modern Chinese antenna.

Gilding, brilliant color, and awnings bearing religious symbols are common features of Tibetan temples.

The complexity of religious architecture in the Potala is stunning.

The living quarters of the Dalai Lama were at the top of the White Palace. From a private balcony, this god-king could observe religious plays and ceremonies being held in the broad courtyard below.

Monks gather in an airy enclosure at the Potala.

Following Page
As pilgrims approached the holy city of Lhasa, the golden rooftops of the Potala Palace could be seen in the distance.

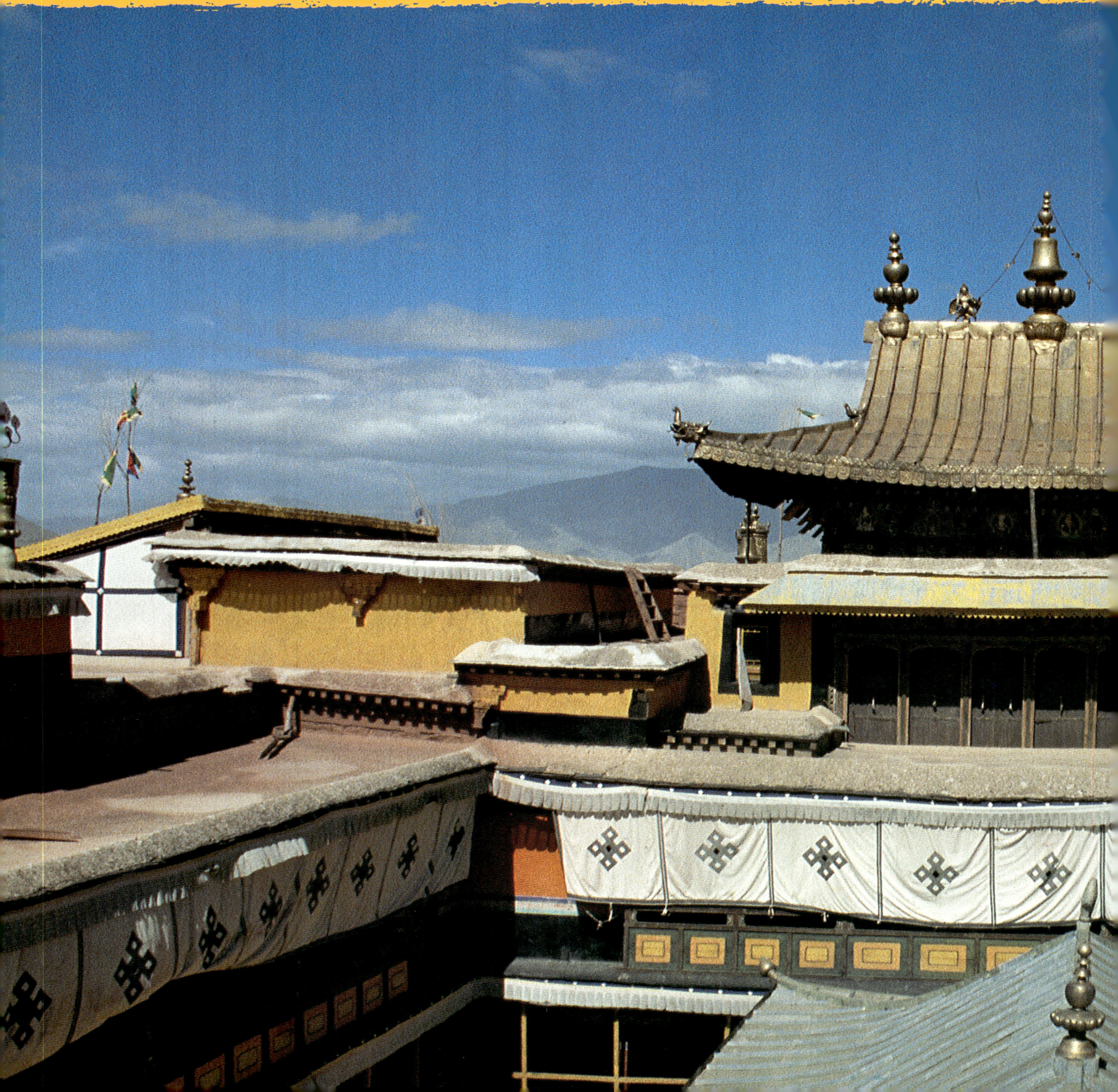

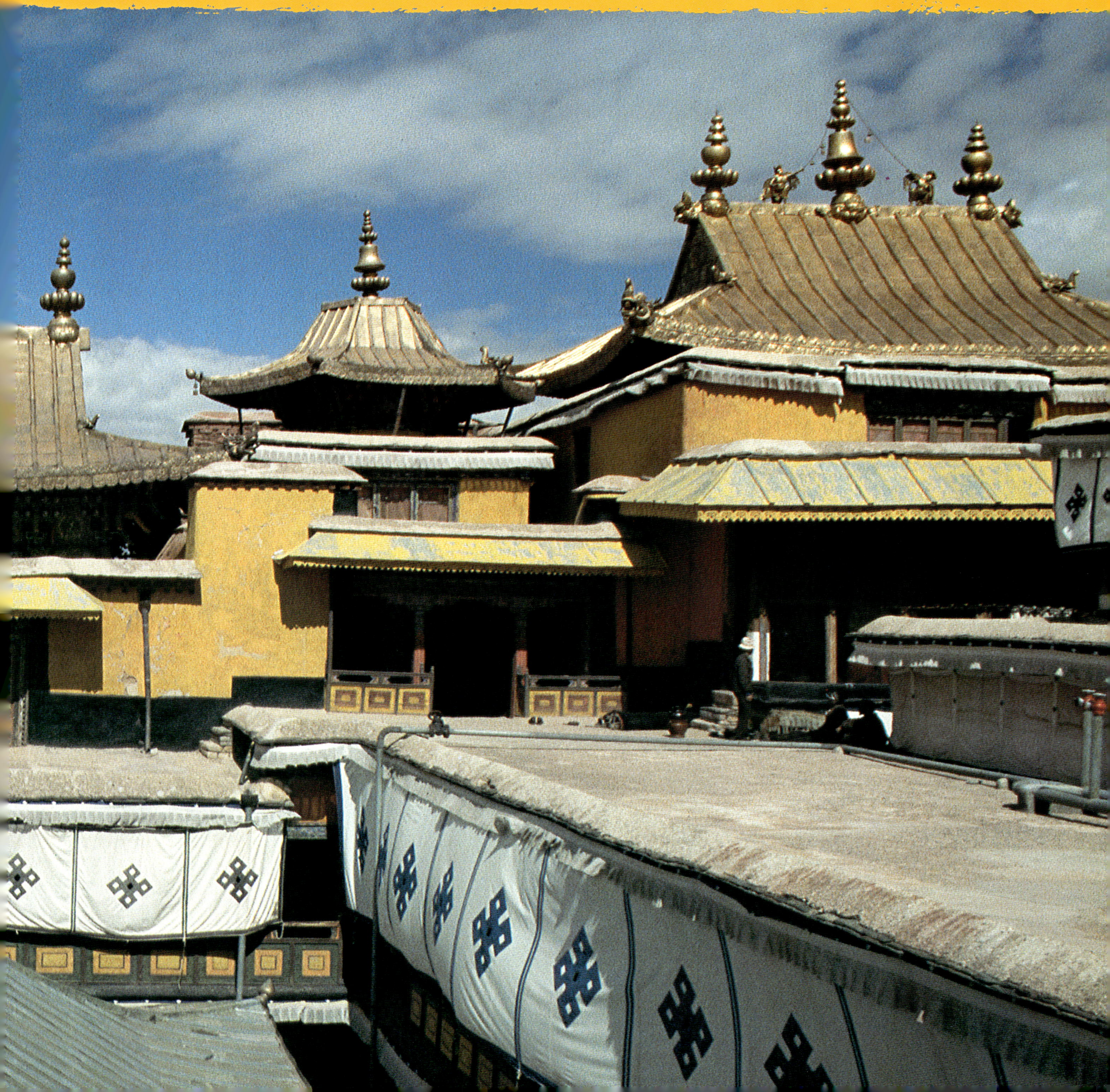

A ferocious bronze griffon decorates a corner post.

Made of braided yak hair, this parasol is symbolic of royalty and the protection of Buddha.

Buddhist monks chant and read from sutras, accompanied by the eerie tones of religious music.

Prayer flags and a small incense burner are added to the religious symbols atop the Potala.

Ahetsangu Nunnery

Pillows cushion the floor of the Ahetsangu chanting hall, surrounded by brightly painted columns and silken hangings.

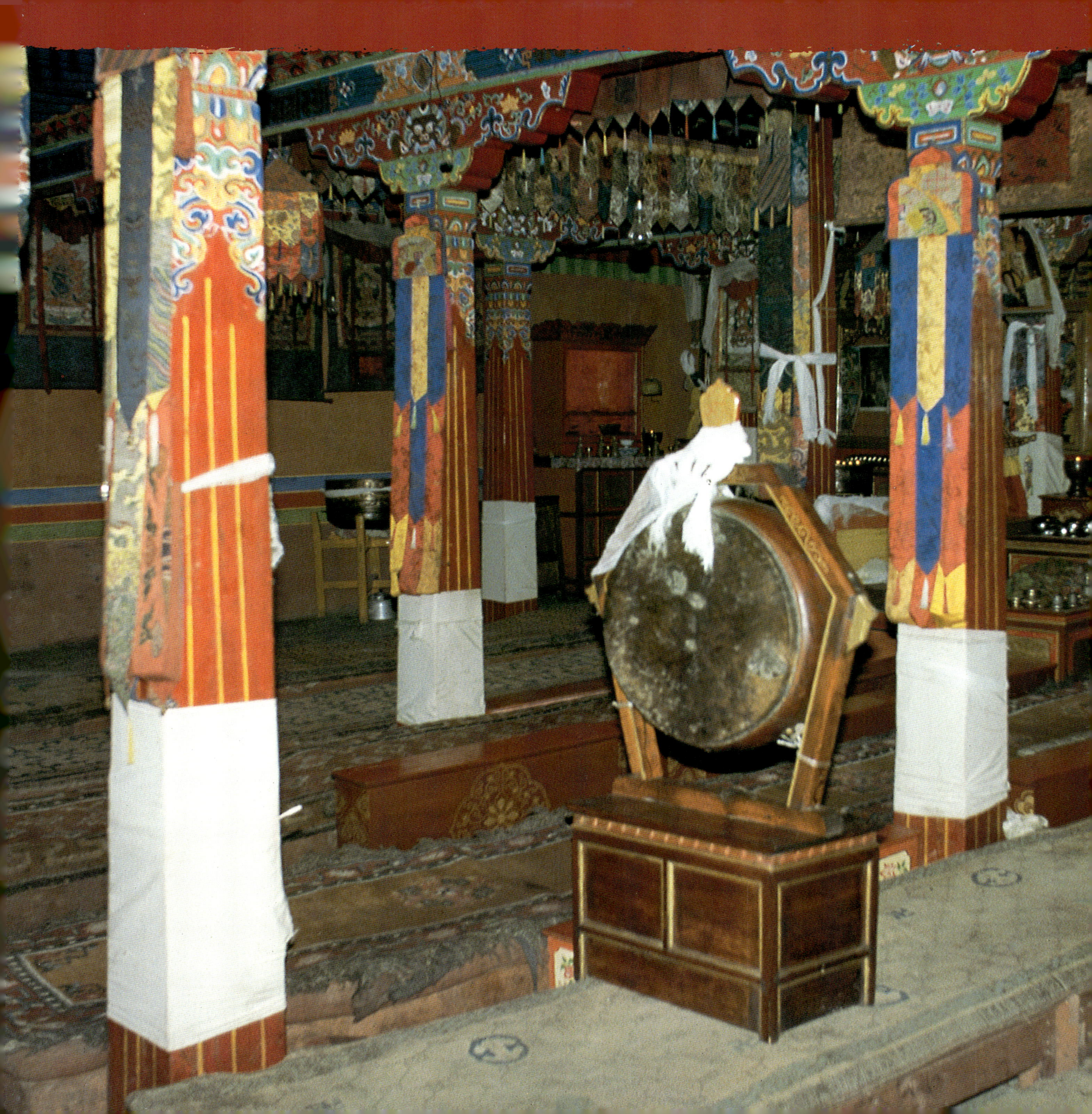

The Barkhor

A group of Tibetan women link arms in friendship as they stroll around the Barkhor in a clockwise Buddhist fashion. Long renowned for their gentle ways, Tibetans must now face the often difficult demands of a modern and still alien world.

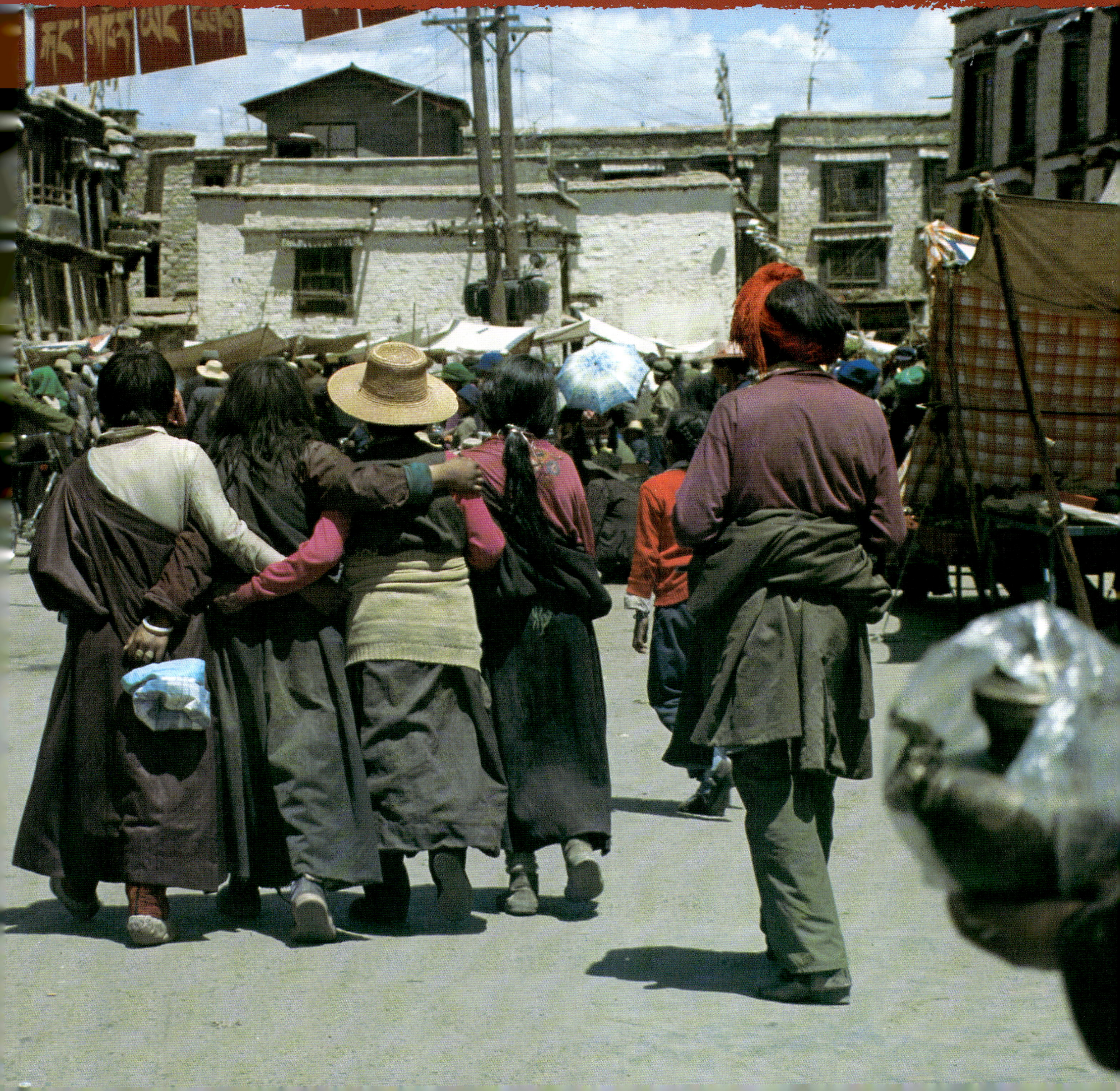

Tibetans are a friendly people, long known for their open gentleness. Her face etched with age and years of exposure to the strong sun of the area, this woman is dressed in traditional clothing.

A vision of timelessness, a Tibetan monk is wrapped in the robes of his monastic order, and wears spectacles of another age.

Garishly colored imports and bolts of material share space with traditional butter lamps and images of Buddha in Tibetan stalls. Though their clothing may reflect Chinese ways, the people persist in their commitment to their religion.

The Barkhor, that ancient ring-road which encircles the Jokhang, is Lhasa's market-place. Here, on a bit of ground, travellers spread their wares, monastic instruments, butter lamps, collections of block-printed prayers.

A wandering old woman and her grandson sit beside their small arrangement of figures, molded from butter and tsampa, the barley meal that is the staple of life in Tibet.

51

With prayer wheel and beads always in motion, a Tibetan man surveys the marketplace from his position on a Barkhor street corner.

Following the Chinese invasion of Tibet in 1950, religious expression was severely discouraged, and the monasteries were closed. Although such repression has been somewhat relaxed recently, many of Tibet's monks must now preach and read prayers on street corners.

53

Jokhang Temple

Prayer wheels are a common feature of Tibetan life. Small, hand-held prayer wheels are evident everywhere, as are long rows of prayer wheels in monasteries or shrines, like these in a Jokhang courtyard. Containing long scrolls of prayers, sutras, they are spun continually by the faithful.

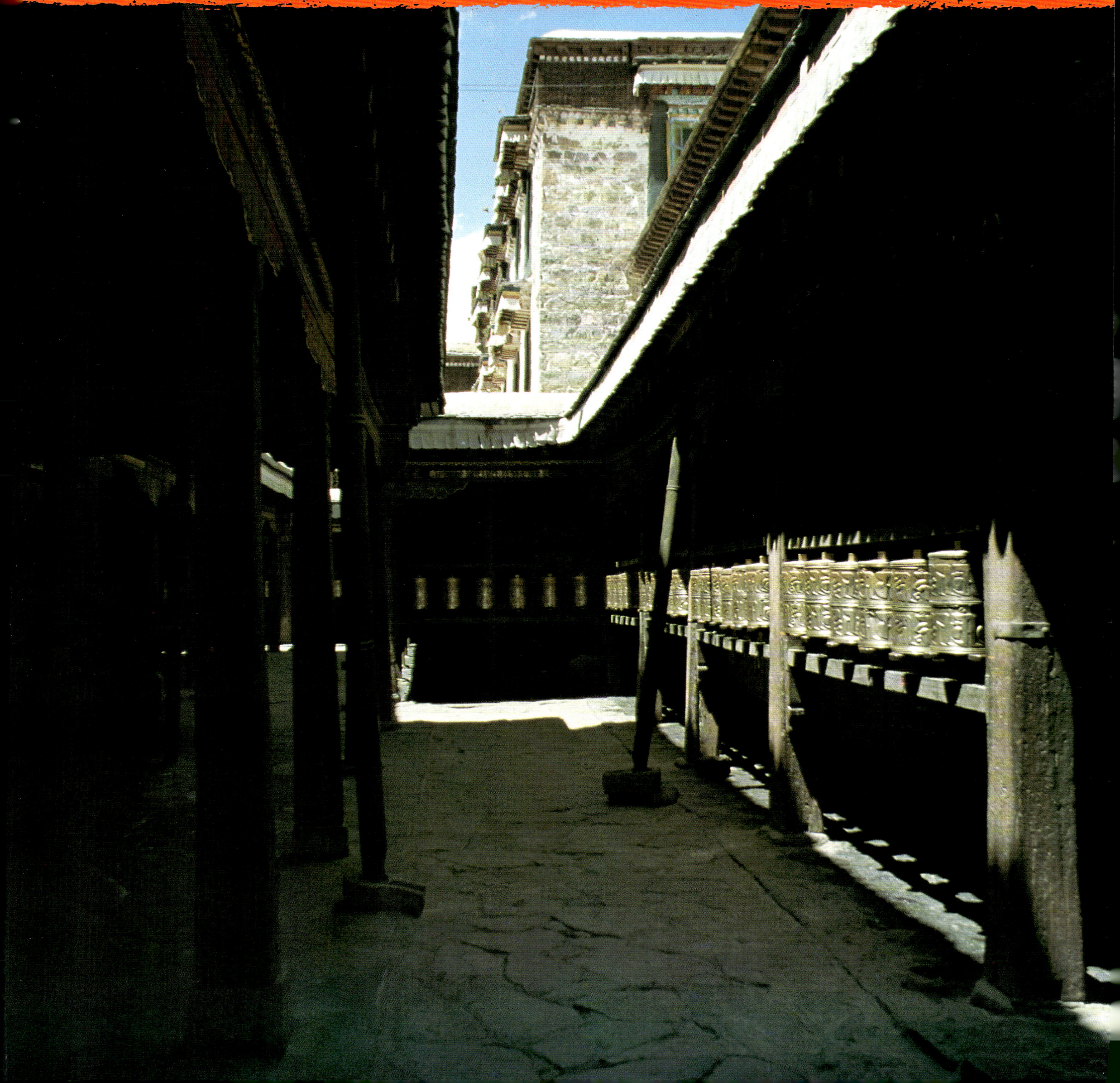

Tibetan stone houses are built cheek-to-jowl in clusters in old Lhasa, quite different from modern buildings constructed by the Chinese.

Reminiscent of early Chinese architectural influence, temple rooftops are elegant in their gilded up-turned eaves and brilliant colors.

Following Page

The Jokhang Temple is a complex, multi-levelled warren of shrines, chambers, workshops, and living quarters. Of traditional Tibetan design, it is ablaze with color.

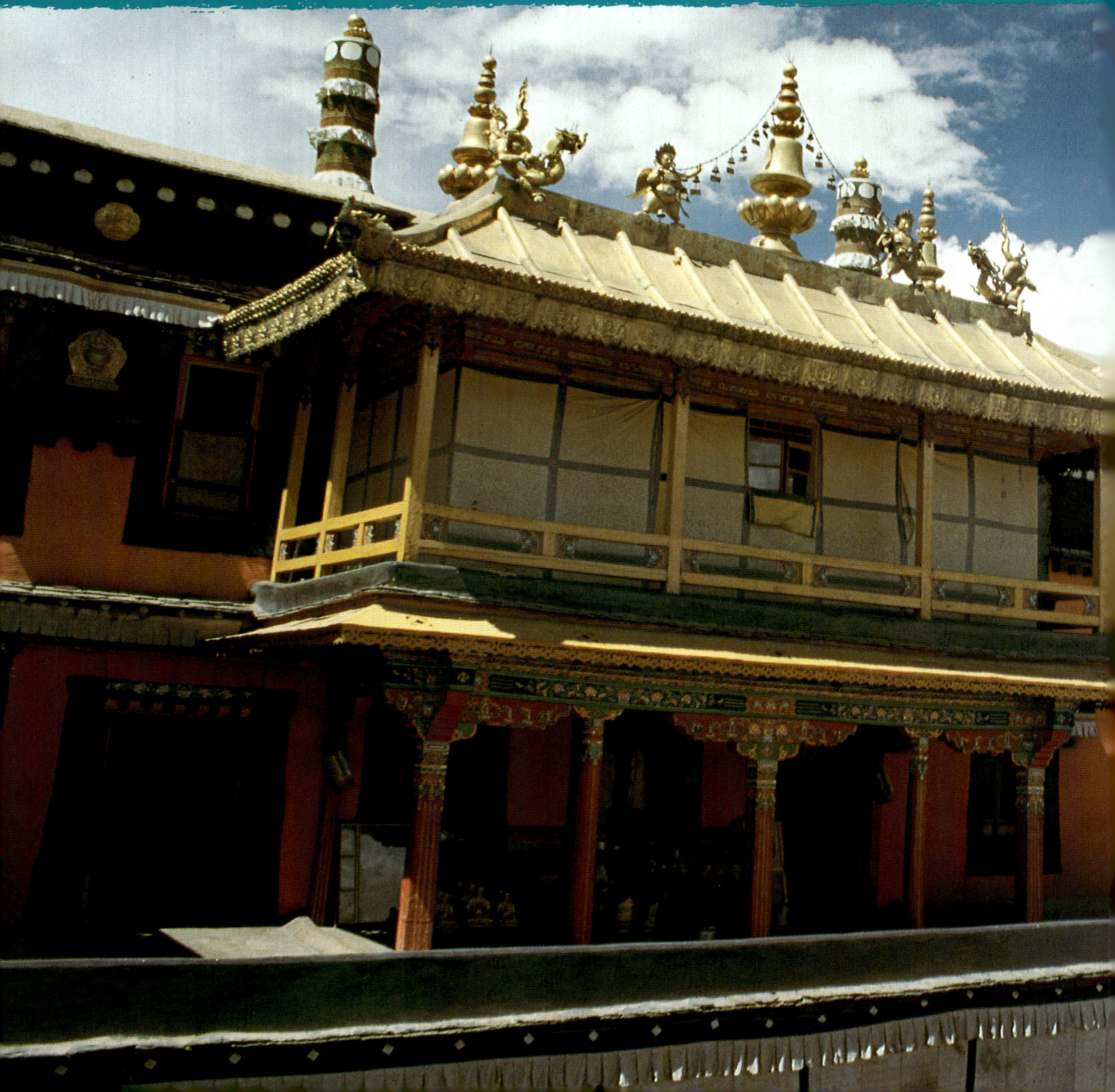

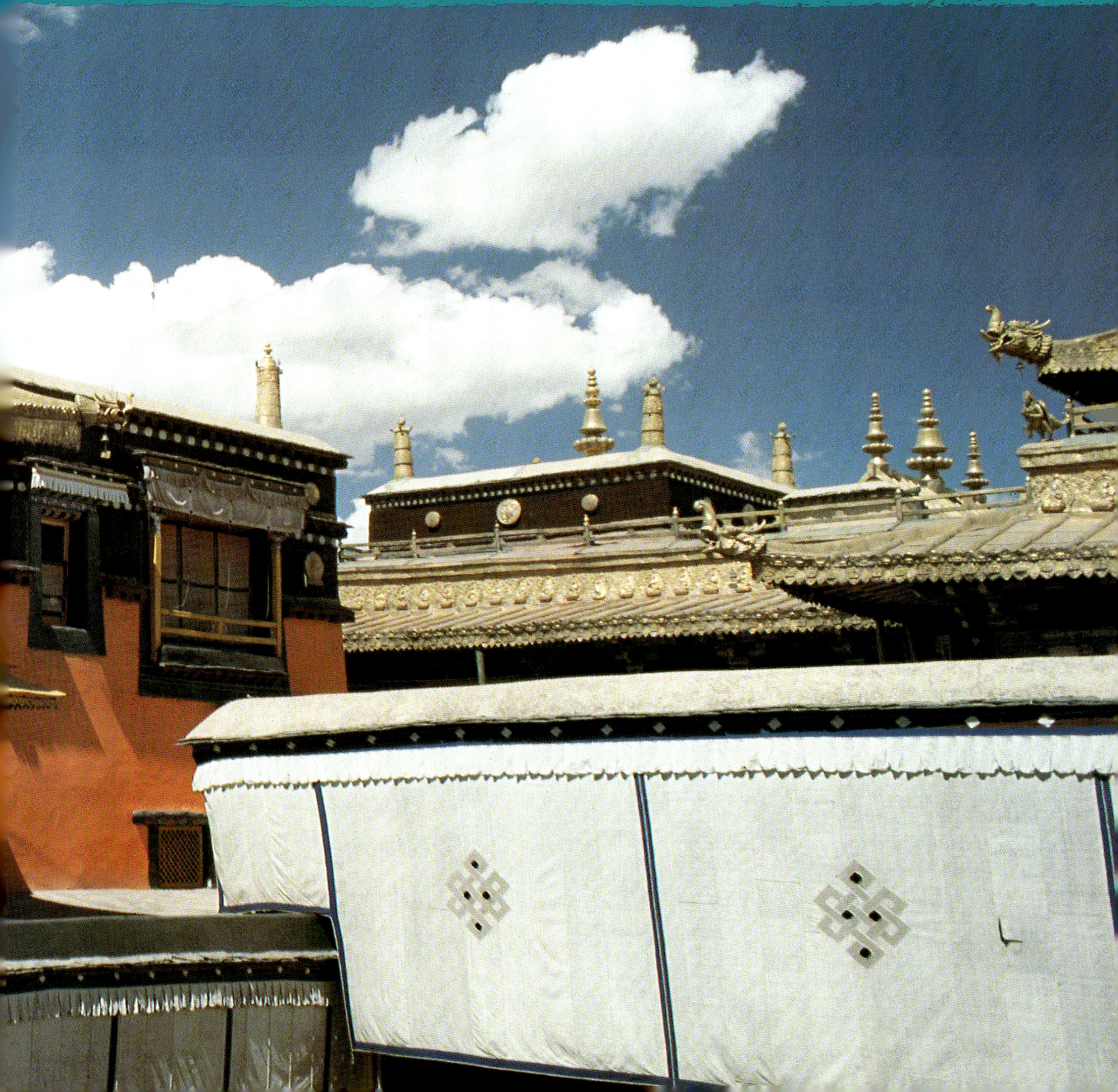

Although sharing no common language, a foreign visitor enjoys meeting young monks at the Jokhang Temple.

Restoration efforts are underway in the courtyard of the Jokhang Temple. Frenzied destruction by Red Guards during China's Cultural Revolution wrought great damage to Tibet's monasteries and shrines.

The Jokhang abounds with religious statuary. Here, a figure of Buddha sits upon a golden throne.

Tibet's national treasure, a gilded and jewelled statue of the Sakyamuni Buddha, sits behind its screen of metal chains in the Jokhang Temple. Over 1300 years old, this statue is revered by Buddhists throughout the country, and pilgrims travel long distances to worship before it at least once in their lifetime.

The doors to Tibet, so long isolated and remote, are now opening and the flood of foreign visitors is sure to continue. An enterprising monk at the Jokhang Temple carries a tape-recorder in his attempt to learn English.

Expressing religious devotion through creative efforts has always been the raison d'etre for many of Tibet's artists. With spectacles tied around his head, and a beard braided into a trailing wisp, this artist works in solitary tranquility as he meticulously paints statues of the Buddha.

Daily Life

Shaggy and powerful, the yak is the backbone of Tibetan life. It not only thrives in the harshest of climates, but provides milk and skins necessary to life in remote areas.

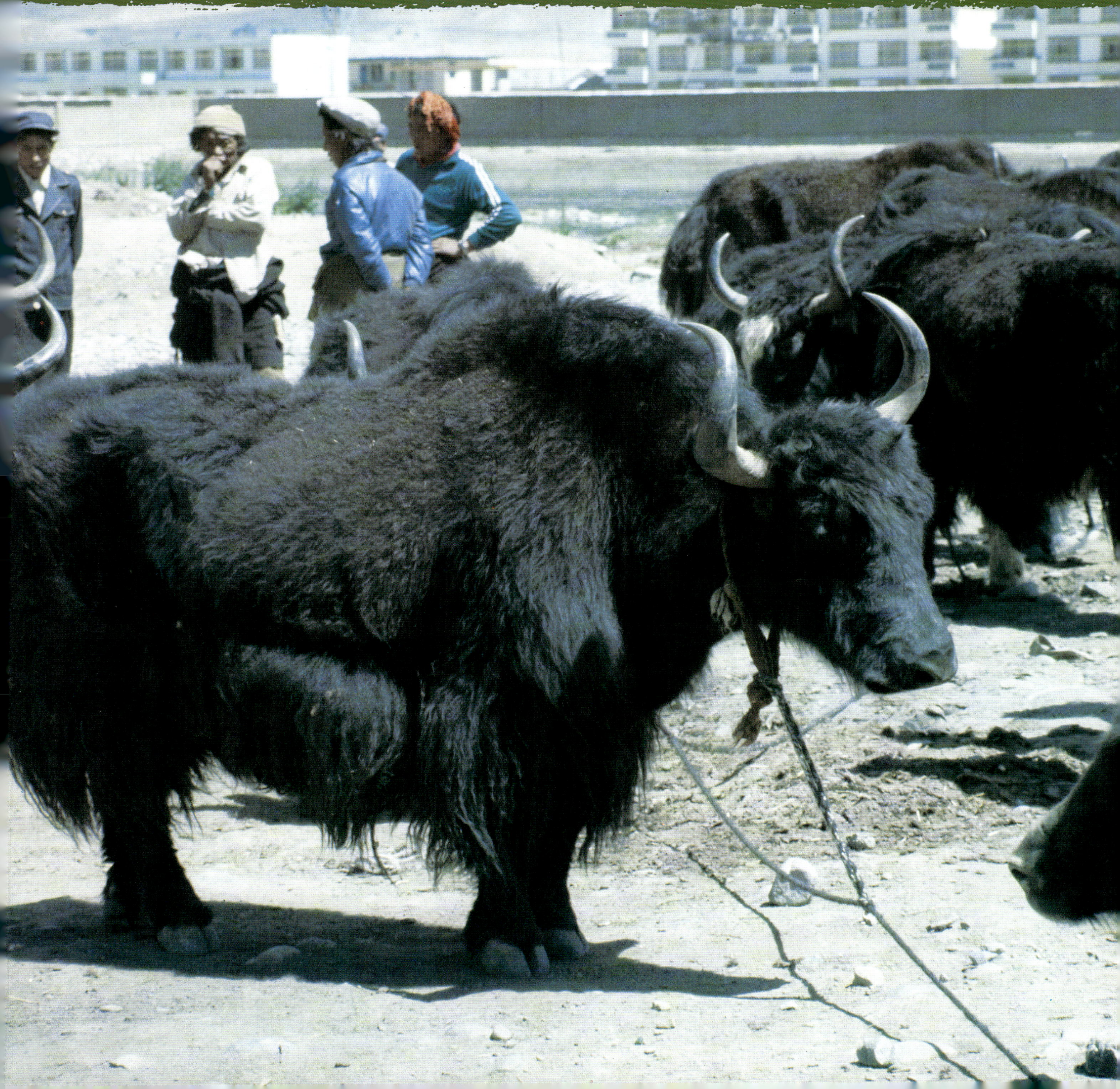

Coracles of primitive design can still be seen on Tibet's rivers.

Called "kowa" in Tibetan, these primitive boats are made of yak hides stretched over a framework of willow branches. Though reasonably sturdy and able to transport people and goods, coracles were designed in antiquity so as to be carried upon the back of a strong man at the end of the voyage.

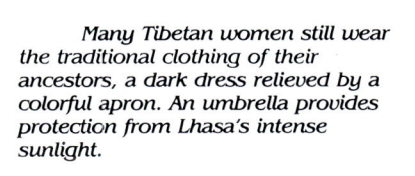

Many Tibetan women still wear the traditional clothing of their ancestors, a dark dress relieved by a colorful apron. An umbrella provides protection from Lhasa's intense sunlight.

A coracle boatman on the Kyichu River.

70

A prayer flag draped suspension bridge leads to Gumolingka Island in the middle of the Kyichu River.

Celestial Burial

To the east of Lhasa is the site of celestial burial. Vultures and other birds of prey swoop down on this rocky outcrop to devour the dismembered pieces of human bodies. A traditional means of releasing the soul of the dead person, celestial burial is still practiced in Tibet.

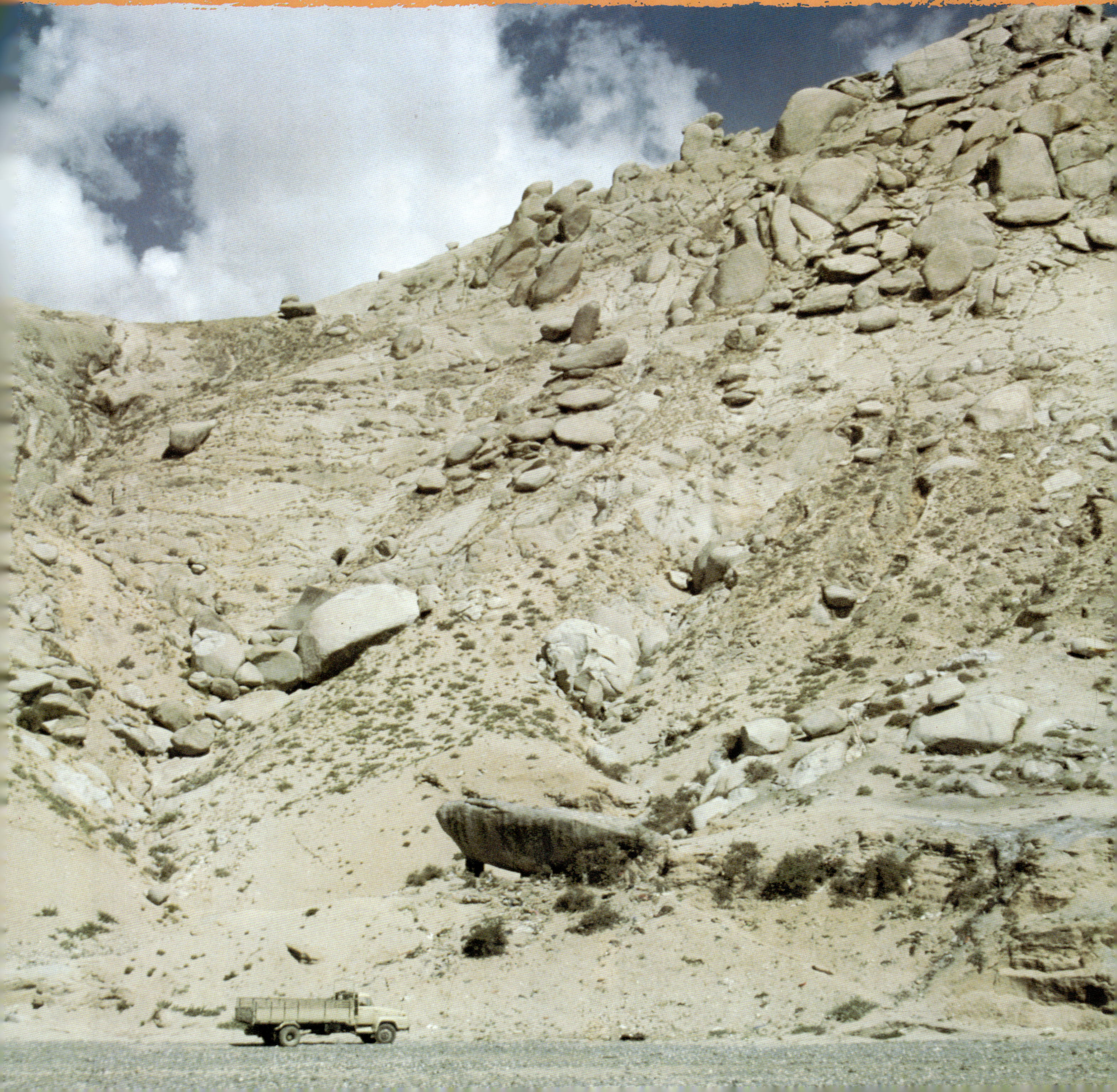

Visitors are unwelcome at the place of celestial burial, a site which is deserted following the dawn rituals.

On the completion of their grim duties, "domdens," or undertakers, sprinkle the rock with tsampa and leave their tools in place.

Drepung Monastery

Tibetan architecture and religious symbolism are combined in the ancient buildings of Lhasa.

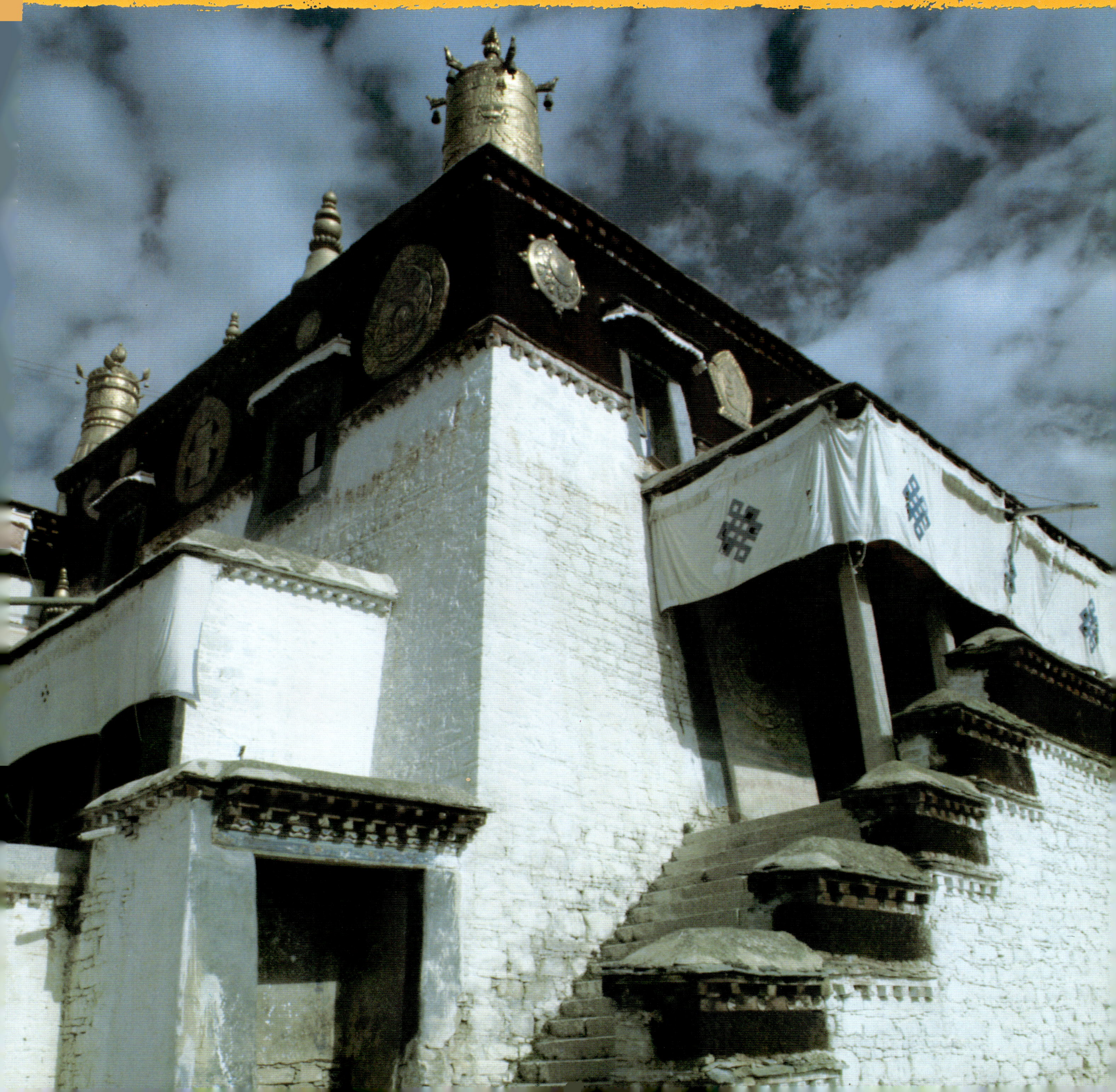

Drepung Monastery sprawls at the foot of Mt. Gyengbuwudze. Once home to 10,000 monks, only a few hundred are allowed to remain today.

Holy Mt. Gyengbuwudze rises at the back of Drepung Monastery. Mystics once dwelt in peaceful isolation in caves hollowed into the mountain, and a temple crowned its highest peak.

Pilgrims visit a Tibetan shrine.

Masters of stone and woodwork, long forgotten Tibetan architects designed these doorways and courtyards.

The kitchens of Tibet's great monasteries once served thousands of monks daily and are large and smoky places.

82

Sacred religious books, block printed or written by hand, have long been accumulated in monastic libraries.

Statue of the Maitreya, the Buddha to Come.

Detail of multi-headed wall-painting, Drepung Monastery.

Mani stones, hand carved with sutras or the universal mantra, are always found beside pilgrim pathways or close to religious shrines.

A monk prepares an offering.

Sera Monastery

Traditional appliquéd awnings drape the front of a Sera chanting hall.

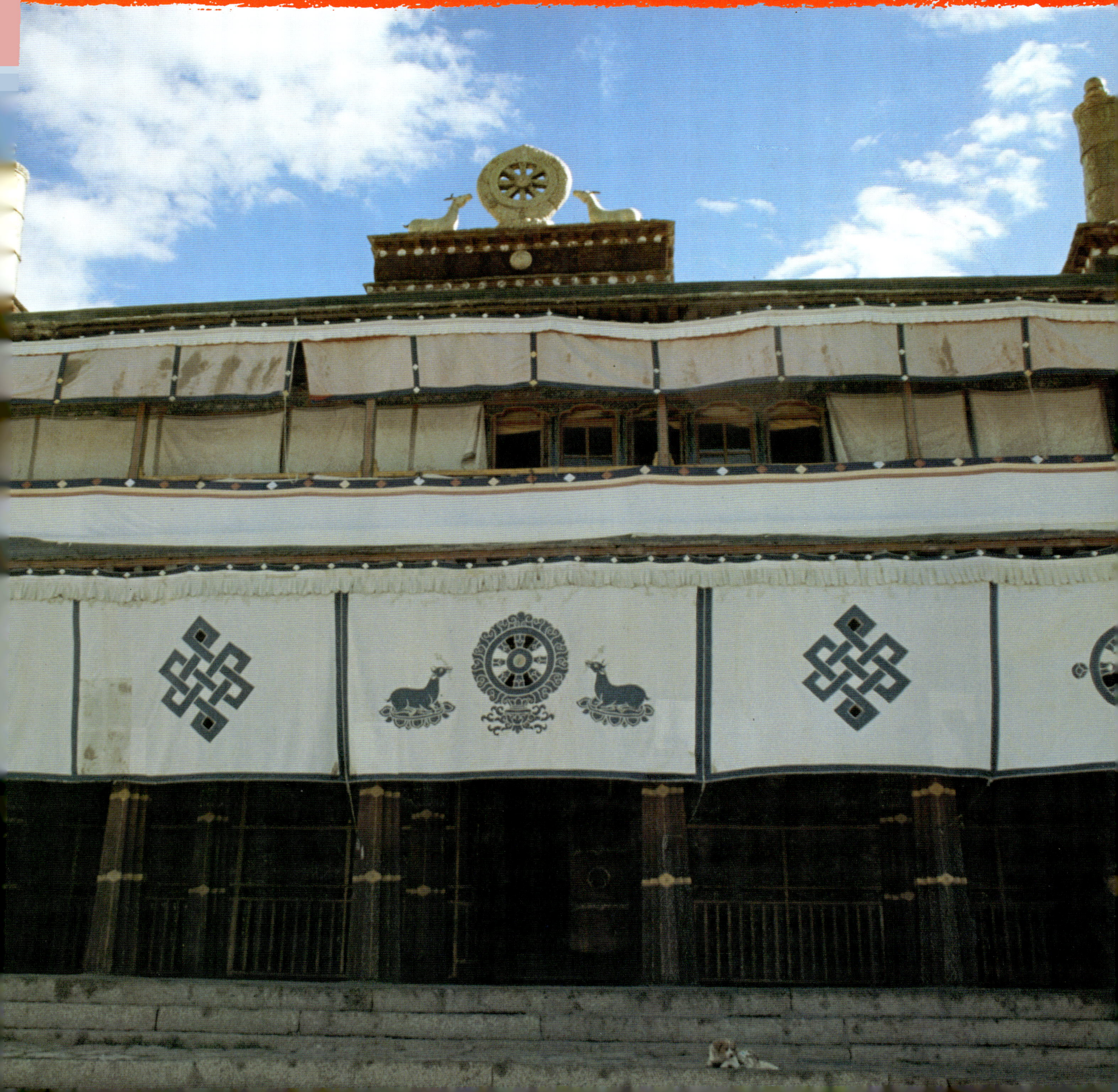

Sera Monastery was a longtime political rival to Drepung's greatness. Its army of feared warrior-monks, the 'dob-dobs,' was formed to reinforce its influence.

Peaceful now in its antiquity, the Tantric monastery of Sera was once a hotbed of intrigue.

Once part of a thriving artistic community, the last of Sera Monastery's great thangka-masters appears on the steps of a communal chanting hall. No longer encouraged as a skill of value in Chinese Tibet, thangka painting is rapidly dying out, but still thrives in Tibetan Buddhist communities in India, Nepal, Sikkim, Bhutan and Ladakh.

In direct contrast to the austere Tibetan landscape, temples are enlivened with brilliant colors and complex ecclesiastical symbolism.

Following Page

Gilded and set with turquoise and coral, a statue of the Buddha reflects tranquility and wisdom.

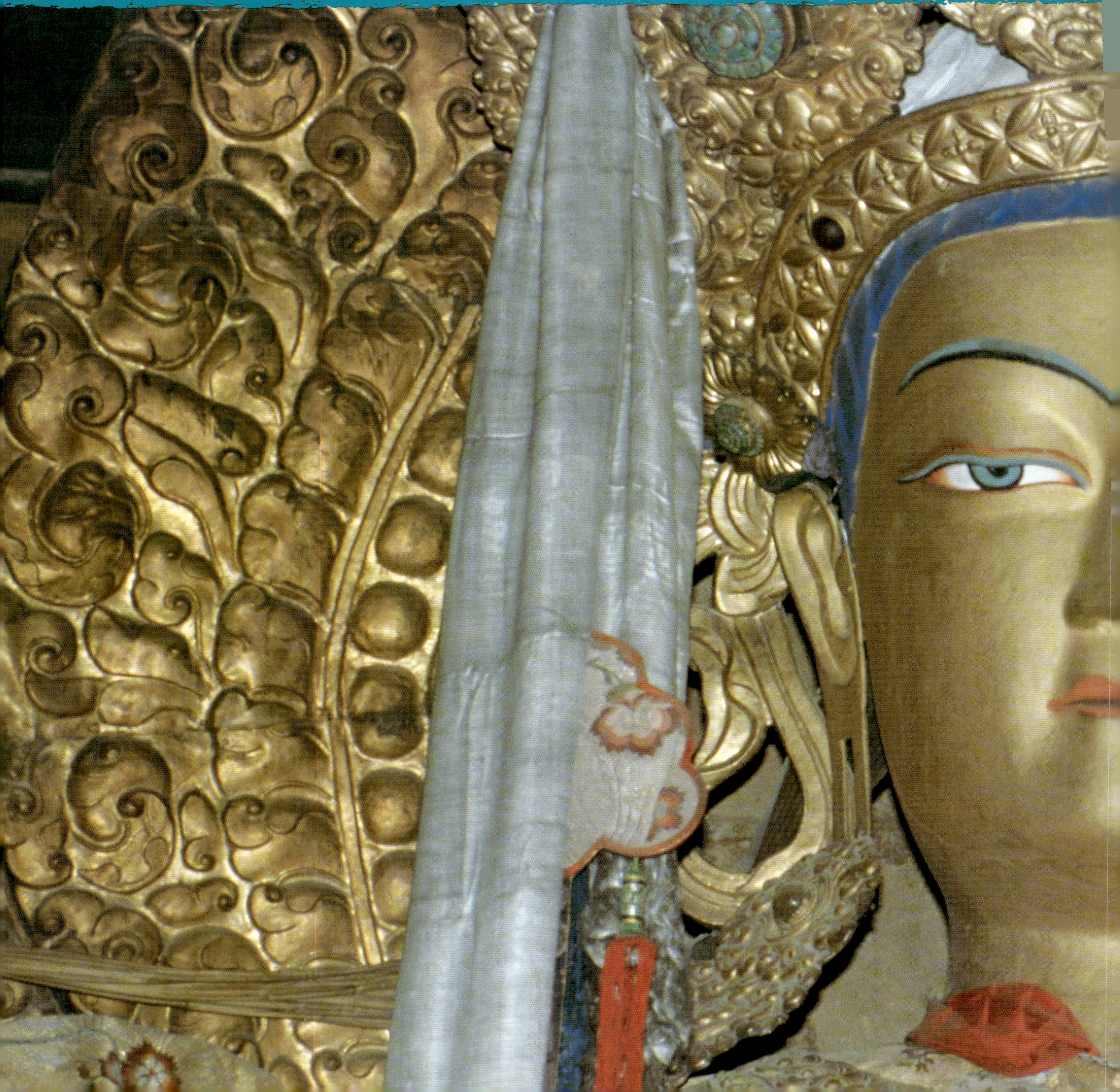

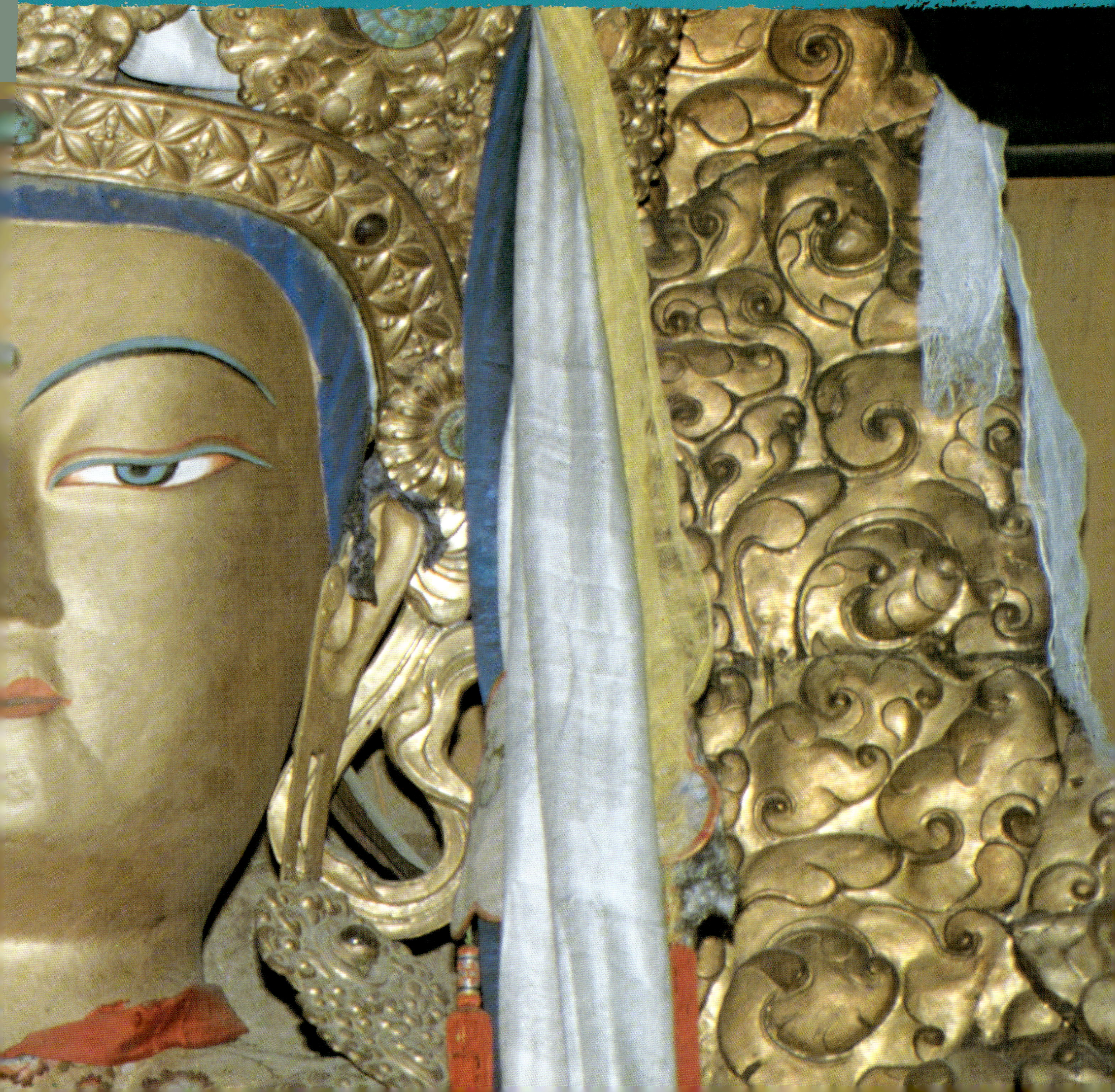

Visitors to Buddhist shrines are often disturbed by the realistic and very menacing appearance of protective statues.

An infinite number of important religious figures appear in Tibetan Buddhist art, and their similarities often make exact identification difficult. Tsong Khapa, the founder of the Yellow Hat sect, is always recognized by his smiling face, long earlobes, and peaked cap.

His face reflecting tranquility and compassion, a massive statue of the Buddha is draped with white khata scarves.

In a wall mural at Sera Monastery, the Sakyamuni Buddha is portrayed at the center of all existence.

A monk carries a smoking incense burner.

In one of the oldest chambers at Sera Monastery, a solitary monk accompanies his prayers with the ritual beating of cymbals and tapping of a drum.

A young monk reads from sutras at Sera Monastery.

Tibetan children stand before a throne at Sera Monastery reserved for the holy Dalai Lama. In his absence, a Yellow Sect cap and khata scarves occupy this place of honor.

103

Summer Palace Norbulingka

Built not long before his flight to India, the summer home of the current Dalai Lama is now considered a sacred shrine.

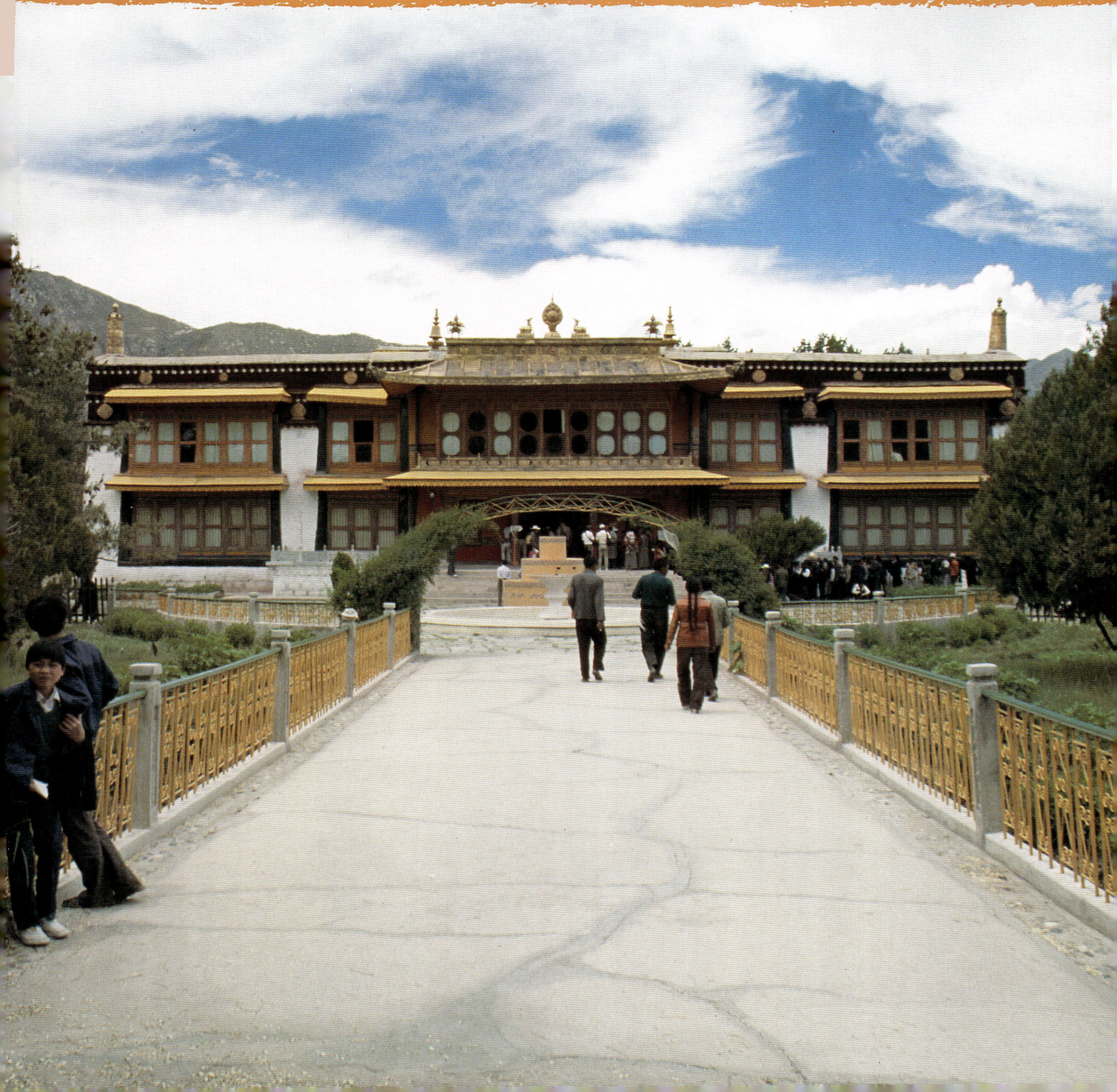

As in all Buddhist shrines, pilgrims will complete their visit to the summer home of the Dalai Lama by circumnavigating the building in clockwise fashion.

Wearing heavy handmade boots and sheep-skin lined "chuba" cloaks, ordinary travellers from eastern Tibet visit the Norbulingka, something forbidden to all but the very few before 1959.

Yak hair and prayer streamers are braided together to form a traditional decoration in this detail from a temple door.

Intricately painted palace doorway at the Norbulingka.